THE STRUGGLE FOR JUSTICE

CONVERSATIONS WITH JOHN BOTTOMLEY ABOUT TRANSFORMING CHURCH COMMUNITY SERVICES

KATE DEMPSEY

COVENTRY PRESS

Published in Australia by
Coventry Press
33 Scoresby Road
Bayswater Vic. 3153
Australia

ISBN 9780648725169

Cataloguing-in-Publication entry is available from the National Library of
Australia http://catalogue.nla.gov.au/.

Cover design by Ian James - www.jgd.com.au
Cover image by Andrea Colvin Photography ·
Text design by Megan Low (Filmshot Graphics FSG)
Formatted in Amerigo

Printed in Australia

CONTENTS

"I hate, I despise your religious feasts;
I cannot stand your assemblies.

Even though you bring me burnt offerings and grain offerings,
I will not accept them.
Though you bring choice fellowship offerings,
I will have no regard for them.

Away with the noise of your songs!
I will not listen to the music of your harps.

But let justice roll on like a river,
righteousness like a never-failing stream!"

See Amos 5:21-24

PREFACE

In 1994, I was engaged as a consultant by the Uniting Church Synod (Commission for Mission) to undertake a review of the church's disability, child, youth and family welfare policy. I produced a discussion paper to address the call for a greater sense of direction and purpose and to discuss the work of community services agencies in the wider ministry of justice and service of the Uniting Church. That report some 25 years ago is noted in this book and the author, Kate Dempsey, comments that what I called the 'twin challenges of rediscovering the gospel in the midst of our work and rediscovering the place of mission in our faith communities' remains today.

This book gives us an opportunity to revisit the big questions that underpin our work and our faith. It asks us to take the time to consider if what we are doing does indeed bring about more justice into the world. It does so through the work of Revd John Bottomley and the Creative Ministries Network, one of the founding agencies of Uniting. It is an important resource for anyone wanting to understand the work of the Creative Ministries Network; its history and the breadth of reports, studies, research and advocacy it engaged in and the issues that it canvassed over its 40-year history (together with its predecessor agencies).

This book takes the standpoint of a conversation between John Bottomley and the book's author, Kate Dempsey, as they develop a shared language for describing the difficult questions that have and continue to face community services in Australia: questions regarding the dignity and respect of persons and what John calls the 'disease of modernity' which reduces people to mere commodities to be traded and consumed. There is much to value in John's reflections on the place of work in our lives, the orthodoxy of self-interest notable in discourse today and the ongoing impact of how Australia was colonised.

John and Kate have invited us into their conversations and thereby given us the opportunity to consider our own path anew, with questions for reflection at the end of each chapter and with outlining a reflection cycle to follow if we so choose. I have had many thoughtful and challenging conversations with John Bottomley over the years and I have found him to be passionate in his desire to see the joining of Word and deed and to make sense of the place of the people of God in relation to the influence of the dominant culture within which we live our lives.

John has a keen sense of his work as a prophetic ministry and has worked tirelessly in his career to call the church to account. We may not agree with all his views, but this book offers an opportunity to renew a dialogue and allows a new audience to consider the key themes of John's writing spanning 40 years and including three books and countless reports.

I am pleased to add this small preface in the hope that staff, consumers and volunteers at Uniting may find it useful as they reflect on the larger questions of the purpose and value of life. I commend it to the broader church to help us all participate further in the dialogue that brings about increasing justice in the world.

Paul Linossier
CEO, Uniting Victoria and Tasmania

DEDICATION

This book is titled *The Struggle for Justice*. The Old Testament prophet, Amos told Israel that God had no interest in their songs, feasts, praise or services while there was injustice in the world. Rather, God called on the people to go out into the world and work to ensure there was justice everywhere. This is what God wants to see – humanity back on track and realising that the world is a beautiful and abundant place and that we have a responsibility to join together to ensure it is safe, fair and just for all who live on it.

The book summarises the ministry and key works of Revd John Bottomley, an ordained Minister of the Word in the Uniting Church in Australia. John has written over 80 reports and three books over his 40-year work history. This book was commissioned by Uniting (the community services organisation of the Uniting Church in Victoria and Tasmania) to commemorate his work and which I undertook with John's support to be a gift for the staff and volunteers who carry Uniting's community services work today. It is, therefore, written as both a summary of John's work and also as 'conversation' between John and me as a means for staff to reflect deeply about the work they do. As an academic and workplace consultant, I write and speak on issues from the viewpoint of political and philosophical thought and I use the concepts of psychoanalysis. Whereas John uses the languages of sociology and theology. This book tries to bring those languages together. Each chapter has questions for reflection at its conclusion; these may be studied alone or used to aid reflection in staff retreats, meetings, conferences and the like. A cycle of reflection is introduced and discussed to support both personal and group reflection. It is reproduced below and discussed in some detail in chapter five, *Finding the Liminal Space*.

I dedicate the book to John and to Margaret Neith and to the very large group of those who were involved in the work of the Urban Ministry Network, the Centre for Creative Ministries and the Creative Ministries Network over the years, including many researchers, staff, clients, board members, ministers, friends, volunteers, funders and supporters of the mission in the three agencies that John Bottomley worked with since 1984.

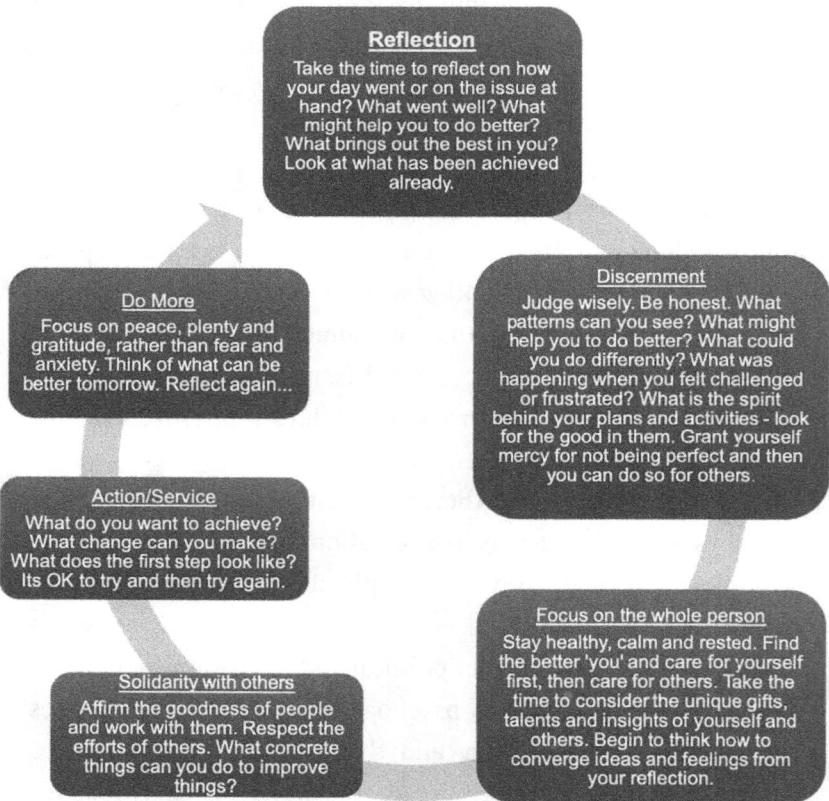

Reflection
Take the time to reflect on how your day went or on the issue at hand? What went well? What might help you to do better? What brings out the best in you? Look at what has been achieved already.

Do More
Focus on peace, plenty and gratitude, rather than fear and anxiety. Think of what can be better tomorrow. Reflect again...

Discernment
Judge wisely. Be honest. What patterns can you see? What might help you to do better? What could you do differently? What was happening when you felt challenged or frustrated? What is the spirit behind your plans and activities - look for the good in them. Grant yourself mercy for not being perfect and then you can do so for others.

Action/Service
What do you want to achieve? What change can you make? What does the first step look like? Its OK to try and then try again.

Focus on the whole person
Stay healthy, calm and rested. Find the better 'you' and care for yourself first, then care for others. Take the time to consider the unique gifts, talents and insights of yourself and others. Begin to think how to converge ideas and feelings from your reflection.

Solidarity with others
Affirm the goodness of people and work with them. Respect the efforts of others. What concrete things can you do to improve things?

Figure1 Reflection Cycle used in this book.

AUTHOR'S INTRODUCTION

In the early 1980s, I was working at the State Government Offices in Cranbourne (South East of Melbourne). In those days, Cranbourne was still really a country town; now it is a suburb of the great metropolis of Melbourne. I worked from an office above a real estate agent shop in the High Street.

My employers were the thirteen local government authorities that made up the Westernport Region. I was examining ways to improve employment opportunities and create jobs for local people in a rapidly changing economy. It was a time of economic recession and significant transformation of manufacturing industries including the removal of trade barriers whose removal we take for granted today. As whole industries declined –particularly textiles, clothing and footwear manufacture, car manufacturing, metal work and other traditional trades– governments began funding efforts to re-train redundant workers and create new industries to take their place. The Westernport area was hard hit by both the recession and the industry re-structuring occurring at the time and so I was employed to assist.

Through this work, I met Margaret Neith, the Planning Officer at nearby Dandenong TAFE College (now Chisholm Institute). Margaret asked me to meet and discuss employment issues with her husband who was undertaking research on working life for the Combined Union Shop Committee at Williamstown Naval Dockyard. This is how I met John Bottomley. We had a chat, found we had an interest in social research in common and that we had a strong desire to consider the larger questions in life. I did not know when I met him, that John was an Ordained

Minister of the Word in the Uniting Church.

It was the start of a friendship and collaboration of over thirty-five years. Since our meeting, John and I have had regular weekly lunches, we have worked together, we have co-authored papers and given workshops together. I was on the board of the Urban Ministry Network, founded by John and others in the 1990s and later I was Chairperson of the Board of its ultimate successor, the Creative Ministries Network, at the time it was closed down by the Synod Standing Committee before its community service program was absorbed into Uniting in 2016.

This book describes John's work and the development of his thinking over forty years. It summarises the key learnings from John's collaborations with many others including myself over his working life and as part of the agencies he created to research theology and working life.

John was never a 'typical' parish Minister. From the time I knew him, he was in secular employment, trying to assist those at the margins of our society by using research, social justice programs and services of public worship to bring the voice of disenfranchisement to the awareness of those with the power and the funds to assist. When we first met, he was researching working rights. He later went on to investigate workplace death and injury. Most of his professional life has been focused on those at the margins of working life. He has always been interested in finding creative ways both to research and to express the powerlessness of those who are losers in our modern game of winner and losers.

He created and/or operated three main entities for the expression of his work, after pioneering research with Margaret on women's work in the home in his first parish at Scoresby

Uniting. The three entities were the Urban Ministry Network, followed by the Centre for Creative Ministries, which later merged to become the Creative Ministries Network. In this book, I will discuss each of these agencies and John's work within them.

Towards the end of John's working life, the Creative Ministries Network became an agency of the Uniting Church with John's support and activism. It was auspiced by the Synod of Victoria and Tasmania as a UnitingCare agency and gained access to some project funding from the Synod and John's former parish of St George's East St Kilda in the early 2000s. In 2016, it was absorbed into a new community service entity within the Church called Uniting and lost its independence. This book was commissioned by Uniting to gather the history of the agency and John Bottomley's work so they may continue to bring the need for justice in working life to the agenda of the new agency.

John and Margaret are two of my closest friends. When I met John, it was in his capacity as a social researcher. It is true that John has a theological perspective on the large questions of life and I do not. Nevertheless, we have found that while we speak a different 'language', we are often in agreement about the root cause of pain and suffering in our world today.

For John, it is about us having forgotten that we were created in love by a God who only desires our gratitude for the gift of our lives and that our gratitude is demonstrated in good relationship – with God, each other and the earth. Instead, we have become caught up in a game of 'winners and losers' where we worry about scarcity; put a price on everything and see ourselves as individuals with rights, rather than social beings with responsibilities to look after each other. We have lost a sense of community.

I would put it that we have lost our way because of the commodification of everything; of the seeping of the market view of the world into every sphere of action. For me, post-capitalist economies have leached our political and public life of any moral compass. The game of 'winners and losers' has become the only game we play now and it isolates us from each other, it punishes those who are not able to 'win' and it means we separate our personal and family lives from our public or professional lives.

John and I agree on two fundamental ideas: (1) the primacy of the language of economics nowadays has become the prevailing means of describing our humanity and (2) that this is to our personal and collective detriment. I think I can confidently say that both John and I would agree that the focus on individual rights, the (perceived) scarcity of goods and the sense of competition for those scarce goods has led to a sorry state where as a society we are captured by the dominant ideology (a group of values and beliefs that are not necessarily true) and are only able to think first and foremost of our own needs rather than those of others. It has led us to accept situations, unthinkingly and unquestioningly, which are simply untenable for life on this planet.

There is a sad race to the bottom where *those who have* greedily hang on to what they have with fear that it may be taken from them at any moment; and *those who do not have* seek any means possible to join the winners club or simply give up and became isolated, homeless or mentally ill. Perhaps individualism has finally triumphed: each person competes for scarce resources and feels responsible only for themselves or direct family members. The corollary is that we ruin the earth without any ability to see what we are doing, and we blame those who are losers in the game – as if it is their own fault for having a disability, being a refugee, having an accident at work, and they are often seen as not 'worthy' of our assistance and in fact they are of no value in and of themselves. Such people are not 'productive' members of our economy. They do not deserve support. In our society, only those who work hard deserve their rewards.

We see this attitude in tax cuts to the rich because that will lead to job creation (generally proved wrong, but government's still argue for it), maintaining social security benefits at a low rate because otherwise it discourages those receiving benefits from getting a job, not welcoming refugees as they will 'take our jobs'. We even see it in the argument that those of us without children should not have to pay for childcare (through taxes) since they do not have children. We have profit-making companies operating our gaols and detention centres; we have profit at the heart of building roads, welfare and aged services and hospitals. Our bizarre focus on money causes us to think it is fine for the rich to avoid paying their fair share of taxes, to merely shrug when we read of scandals in the banking sector, to assume it is absolutely fine for a business that pollutes the earth to simply pay a fine and continue to pollute.

Whatever the cause, it seems to both John and me that we have lost our way. As philosopher Michael Sandel (2012:6) writes, *today the logic of buying and selling no longer applies to material goods alone but increasingly governs the whole of life. It is time to ask whether we want to live this way.*

A large part of John's life's work involved research of, and responses to peoples' employment and working lives. In today's environment, playing the game of winners and losers in our working life means that maintaining a sense of vocation is hard. It is hard not to see everything as a competition and those we work with and for, as competitors. The emphasis, therefore, is on 'outputs' which can be seen and measured by others (because these demonstrate our ability to win) and thus we emphasise quick and temporary outputs, but not lasting social change for the benefit of others. It is every person for themself. Accompanying this sense of self is identify maintenance (we avoid taking blame or apologising); we self-promote, we look out for 'number one'.

Work itself has also become more akin to this game of winners and losers. We endure short-term contracts, we move from place to place, we have shifting and only temporary relationships at work. Tendering is the norm in business now, accompanied by cost-cutting to the lowest possible figure, and considering workers as 'self-employed contractors' to avoid paying reasonable rates of pay, as well as outsourcing to anonymous, poorly paid workers in developing countries.

All of these developments mean we tend not to focus on long-term change, but on doing whatever is needed to keep the job. We endure tedious, hostile and even dangerous working conditions and we can become cynical and detached from what we are actually doing every day. The sociologist, Emile Durkheim called this situation *Anomie*: the breakdown of standards and values causing individuals to be cast adrift and suffer anxiety from a sense of a loss of ideals and purpose. The biblical prophets call this 'sin' (see Amos 1 & 2); the turning away from God's abundant and good creation and forgetting the source of our being, while turning towards a world of our own creation and in it productive work, where 'I' am at the centre.

Economic rationality (also called neoliberalism) is the dominant discourse in the west and with it comes the idea from Enlightenment times of humanity as heroic individuals who tame, subdue and control the environment. This belief system may be seen in the colonising explorations of the sixteenth and seventeenth centuries that led to the invasion of Australian Indigenous people's way of life. This fundamental injustice in Australia today is what makes Amos' desire for justice to roll on like a river such a potent message for both John and me.

It challenges a way of thinking that leads to the promotion of concepts such as entrepreneurship, flexibility and mobility (which can be deadly in working life) as absolutes.

We are consistently asked to believe that this way of thinking leads to maximising our options for achieving enriched and empowered individual lives, whereas employees are increasingly more likely to suffer short-term insecure contract work (Sennett 1998), a transactional view of relationship and loss of connectedness to organisations and community. This is what John writes about: the notion of the heroic individual privileged over that of the connected social being, leading to a sense of being cast adrift. Sennett (2006) argues that as humans, we are driven to create life narratives for ourselves and in which work plays a major part in our sense of ourselves and our unfolding lives, but short-term transitory work undermines the values of trust, loyalty, commitment and obligation to others.

This book makes it clear that both John and I adopt a critical stance in relation to the dominant western worldview and its belief in the virtue of global free-markets. We think these beliefs have come at a cost and that they seem to stimulate a stark either/or focus. We either accept that the market economy and the way we live now in the West, are good and anything other way of life is not possible or somehow wrong. But it is not 'all good' to have a belief in God and God's justice and 'all bad' to have a committed belief in a free-market capitalist economy. To posit one belief as 'all good' and its opposite as 'all bad' is binary thinking. I discuss this notion of binary thinking in later chapters of this book.

The danger of binary thinking is exemplified is considering work as simply money-making or as a vocation. People may simply work to succeed or believe they have a vocation on the other hand. But these are not necessarily binary opposites. A vocation may engage our hearts, not just our intellect. We feel we are called to join, get involved and assist in making a given situation better. We focus on slow developmental changes for the general good. We work tirelessly for and with others for the betterment of all, and we are dedicated to the cause we follow. But there is a level of complexity and a 'shadow' to believing we work in a vocation, that is rarely discussed.

Let's examine the idea of the competitive and autonomous self versus the idea of having a vocation[1] as an example. The value of being competitive at work is that it gives each of us a goal to strive for and energy to push for what we want. It encourages self-actualisation, fast solutions and growth and it discourages defeatism and depression. On the other hand, it can also lead to cynicism about lasting change for the better and to cutting corners to get to the destination. In contrast, to believe we are working for God's justice as if we have a vocation, may mean we can become stuck in a mindset of having the correct answer to any issue, to be so dedicated that other ways to achieve a goal are not seen as viable. We can become fanatical, and this can lead to a culture of exploitation and burn out.

Believing we have a vocation also has the potential to allow a sense of rightness to flourish; the caring professional can come to believe she/he knows best what is in the client's best interest. It can lead to a lack of desire to learn and grow and to become too comfortable with what we know and how we do things. It can create a sense of superiority, and, perversely, create boundaries and long held grudges against those who do not see 'the truth' associated with the way we see matters.

---

1   I mean here vocation as it is commonly understood, not as a theological concept, but as a sense that work should be a worthy endeavour for the betterment of others.

In summary, there can be both good and unhelpful aspects either to living only for ourselves or working for others. It is not really a situation of one or the other. This type of rigid thinking, where something is either right or wrong with no nuance or grey in between, is stifling and discourages us from thinking deeply. It is not 'all good' to believe we have a vocation and 'all bad' to simply work for the competitive self. With each binary view comes both good and bad. One of the hallmarks of economic rationalism and the prevailing belief system of western economies is based on this notion of binary thinking.

This book takes up the issue of binaries and argues that binary thinking is harming our societies and thereby our planet. We are more than simply economic creatures who buy and sell; we are more than merely competitive and selfish. We are both economic and social; we are both selfish and selfless. We enact our lives across both the public and private realms. We are more than 'one or the other' – we are both and more. There is an abundance and creativity that flows from this realisation, which we can keep in the forefront of our minds as we work to make the world a better place.

+ + + + +

John took up the problem of binaries in the Uniting Church's community services in his 2007 study of ten Uniting Church community service agency CEOs, *In but not of the world.* The study identifies the issues facing agencies and their leaders as an *'ongoing conflict between God's call to the Church to be partners with Christ in building God's desired kingdom, and the desires of worldly powers to build their own empires'* (Bottomley 2008:1). John asserted that the prevailing economic discourse was capturing the Uniting Church, and he later addressed this idea at some length in his book co-authored with Old Testament Professor, Howard Wallace. The process that the UnitingCare CEOs group took on the journey to the establishment of Uniting was in line with a corporate governance textbook, while John argued, the Synod's role was also sadly bereft of theological enquiry.

In 2016, the Creative Ministries Network (CMN) was caught up in widespread change in the governance of the Church's community services work, despite submissions and protestations from the Board of CMN to the Synod's Project Control Group (PCG). I was the Chair of the Creative Ministries Network at the time and our Board was demoralised by the PCGs unwillingness to engage with the uniqueness of the agency's faith commitment in mission and worship. There was for us a bitter irony in our agency having become a community service agency because it was the only institutional option the Synod had for the original urban ministry, and then finally losing our independence as a theologically-based research 'think tank' on working life. Creative Ministries Network was never truly a community service agency.

The process of bringing all the agencies under a single corporate entity in the name of the Church was instigated by a core group of CEOs but proceeded without any cognisance of the history of the relative power and influence of the faith and business worldviews. In his 2008 report, John wrote that this spiritual blindness *'reflects the comparative privilege of the professional worldview in relation to faith in modern industrial society. The privileged status of professional knowledge in modernity has grown out of the belief in the power of science and technology to master nature, and so fuel society's material progress. The pursuit of material progress is based on the ideology that it would automatically lead to increased happiness for all.'* Ten years later, his comment seems prescient as a summary of the manner in which CMN's theologically-based research into the ideology of work was subsumed into the new entity, Uniting.

It is not the purpose of this book to delve into the reasons for the changes, nor to debate the merits of the new Uniting entity. Suffice to say that CMN had a healthy bank balance, which it was using in a considered fashion to fund ongoing research activities into work issues, particularly work-related injury and work-related death. But for an agency to spend more than it generated in annual income was considered untenable by the Synod committee charged with determining the status of agencies to join the new centralised board. That this expenditure was a deliberate strategic action of the CMN Board at the time was deemed to be 'poor fiscal oversight' and so CMN lost its independence and became one of the founding agencies of Uniting.

At the time that it was brought under control of the Uniting Board, the Creative Ministries Network operated a program called GriefWork. This program had been part funded by the Victorian Workcover Authority for many years and continues to operate now. Its Co-ordinator, Bette Phillips-Campbell, has worked for nearly twenty years with the families of those who are injured or die at work. The work of this program is also described in this book.

An integral part of the holistic vision of Creative Ministries Network's response to injustice at work, Griefwork was the only one of many activities that were brought over into Uniting. Other CMN activities included projects on Restorative Justice, research on the experience of widows of men who died at work, artistic projects with war veterans, projects with local Koori groups, a partnership program with a local congregation to raise funds for post-war reconstruction in Sri Lanka, memorial services and rituals, liturgies, workshops, books and reports on a wide variety of topics.

The agency endeavoured to model new ways of working and thinking and drew together a wide and diverse community of thinkers and supporters. The original entity (Urban Ministry Network) also auspiced 'the Sunday Group' for faith reflection, beginning in 1984. This initiative flourished over the decades and by 2008 CMN had developed its own faith community, which became a new congregation of worship in the Uniting Church. The Creative Ministries Congregation is ongoing and it is the only congregation that is recognised by the Uniting Church in Australia as a congregation begun by an agency and which today meets in members' homes.

I would like to thank Uniting and acknowledge the grant Uniting provided for me to write this book, which summarises John's work. Given the sheer breadth of issues he has taken up over the years, I hope I do justice to this task, and I have tried my best to make his work accessible and useful to a new generation of workers in the hope that the large questions of life that he tackles can be given time in people's busy working lives to ponder and consider.

The chapters of this book outline the key fields of endeavour for John Bottomley, the Creative Ministries Network and its two predecessor agencies, the Urban Ministry Network and the Centre for Creative Ministries. It aims to bring together in one place the fields of endeavour, the key themes and teachings from John's work and that of the agencies and his colleagues over a forty-year period.

Following this introduction, chapter one *A Life of Ministry to the World of Work – John Bottomley's Career* summarises the career of John Bottomley and Appendix 1 offers a brief timeline of his jobs and projects. Chapter two, called *A Consistent Thread,* examines the breadth of topics of his writing and links his ideas with the history of ideas and philosophies that has come before to help give the reader context for the large canvas of the topics John covers in his writing. A list of all reports written by John or produced by the various organisations he was part of is provided in Appendix 2.

Chapter three, *Working on the Church's Margins,* outlines the phases of John's work and describes how his thinking changed and developed over time. Chapter four, *Major Themes,* then summarises the key themes that come from John's writing. His work draws links with history, politics and theology in making the case that the way we live today damages people and relationships. Chapter five, *Finding the Liminal Space*, offers suggestions for readers to reflect on the topics raised in the book and to sit with the uncomfortable feelings they may engender. In the final chapter, *Concluding Thoughts*, I note the mixed feelings with which I grappled in writing the book and my hope that I am able to raise a new audience for John's important ideas.

+ + + + +

While I was undertaking my PhD in 2003-2006, I came across a term that was new to me. It is an Aboriginal word, *dadirri*. Sadly, we have no translation in English for this term. The closest we can come to understanding the word is, perhaps, contemplation. Dadirri is *inner deep listening and quiet still awareness* (Ungunmerr-Baumann 2002). Dadirri is the spirit of waiting and listening closely and deeply – in the moment. It encompasses the sense that the answer will come if we can be patient, wait and genuinely listen with our hearts. I have offered questions and prompts at the end of each chapter in this book to help the reader use the spirit of dadirri to reflect on what John Bottomley's writing might have to say about the reader's current situation.

I offer this book in the spirit of dadirri as a gift to the community service workers of Uniting and to others engaged in the service of healing, justice and reconciliation, in the hope that it helps them to be better connected to the spirit of the important work they do and in deep gratitude to John for his friendship, support and his wisdom over our many years of friendship.

It is with confidence that I offer this summation of the work of Revd John Bottomley as a gift to the Uniting Church in the fervent hope that the insights gained, the ideas put forward, the lessons learned can be put to good use by the Church in its ongoing work of solidarity with the poor and disenfranchised and with engaging in the world of work.

Reflections on the Introduction

This author's introduction describes the working relationship between the author and John Bottomley and notes the critical stance that both take on the prevailing ubiquity of the ideology of the market economy. It also notes the tendency to see issues these days in simple binary terms (black and white, with no room for grey).

- This Introduction asks if vocation still exists in the world of work. What's your view?
- Do you feel you have a vocation? What does that mean for you?
- What do you agree that there are the pros/cons to having a vocation?
- Is your dedication to your work strong or are you more focused on getting ahead in your own life?
- Does having a vocation free you to consider the greater good or simply lead to burnout?
- What are the most important elements in the story of your life?
- What is helpful about focusing on 'outputs' at work?
- Are you frustrated by the focus on outputs that you see around you? What important aspects of work might this focus ignore?
- Do you find the business focus and language at your workplace appropriate or is it alienating?
- What do you do that makes you feel most alive?
- What does dadirri mean to you?

CHAPTER 1

A LIFE OF MINISTRY TO THE WORLD OF WORK
JOHN BOTTOMLEY'S CAREER

"This is a book on health and safety like no other I have ever read. It ranges across theology, Marxism, the Protestant work ethic, and the enlightenment." Doug Cameron

This chapter summarises the career of Revd John Bottomley and the following chapters outline in more detail the key themes of his writings and work. Just after John retired, he launched his book, called *Hard Work Never Killed Anybody*. On 7 May 2015, Senator, The Hon. Doug Cameron Acting Shadow Minister For Employment And Workplace Relations and Shadow Minister For Human Services in the Australian Parliament, launched John Bottomley's book. He told those present he was "gob smacked" by the content, the range and the critique embodied in the book.

The book was the culmination of more than forty years of study, practice, writing and support for people who have suffered injustice in the workplace. In it, John Bottomley critiques modern society using the lens of theology to explore and expose the lie that 'hard work never killed anybody'.

The ironic title, *Hard Work Never Killed Anybody* draws on John's personal experience, the testimony of clients experiencing the death of a loved one or work colleague and John's own reading of Scripture to call on the church to confront the work-related causes of suffering and injustice in the world today. John argues

THE STRUGGLE FOR JUSTICE

that God calls the church today to engage in a ministry of the workplace and thereby to challenge the prevailing view that hard work makes us whole and worthy. He calls on parish ministers, congregations and agency staff to question society's unhealthy norms about working life and also to learn the companioning-pastoral care model of solidarity with those who suffer injustice and to call out as idolatrous the belief in the prevailing economic system as the best and only system we can have on this earth. John believes this is his calling and it has been his life's work.

Hard Work Never Killed Anybody is one of over eighty separate works created, edited, commissioned or auspiced by John Bottomley in his career as both a consultant-social researcher and an Ordained Minister of the Uniting Church. John commenced his working life in parish ministry in the outer suburbs of Melbourne in the mid-1970s. In 1983, he had left full time parish ministry and in 1984 joined with other ministers who were employed in secular work across a range of settings to create the Urban Ministry Network. Its vocational calling was to be in solidarity with people suffering injustice in social and workplace settings; places the traditional church did not readily enter, as the church focused (and still does to this day) primarily on its congregational followers. Later, in 1991, John would return part-time to congregational ministry at St George's East St Kilda Uniting Church and for thirteen years, he worked both within traditional church structures and the evolving agencies he initiated and managed.

For over forty years, John has worked to bring an understanding of workplace harm and injustice and has developed and promoted a huge variety of responses to the suffering witnessed at work, all with a consistent call for justice and reconciliation. He also tried to apply his developing understandings of working life, and his theological insights, to the management and direction of the three agencies' staff and their endeavours.

This book covers the history of John Bottomley's work, outlining the key documents he has created, the broad themes he has traversed and his commitment to modelling his insights within his own workplace, highlighting lessons for others who tread a similar path.

The extent of issues covered by John over his career is breathtaking. He has written on topics as diverse as the impact of colonialist heritage on Australian society, the damage caused by the separation of the public and private spheres of life, prophetic and artistic imagination, new ways of thinking for the church, restorative justice and many other grand themes, all with the commitment to working alongside those who trusted John with their stories and encompassing a cultural and theological critique of the meaning of work in today's world.

In conversation with me while I was writing this book, John told me that as a theological student training for the ordained ministry of the Methodist Church in 1970-72, the world of work was virtually invisible. The primary focus of ministry training was the worship and pastoral care of the residentially-based congregations. With his first parish placement in the growing outer suburbs of Melbourne, John found that the parish church nurtured a privatised faith, focused on home life and the family, while virtually ignoring the public world of paid work.

He began to feel that his training did not equip him to deal with the suffering he saw in his parish, to understand his own emotional response to it, nor did it help him to feel he could respond to it. He tells a poignant story of how he avoided coming to see the family of a dying parishioner because he was 'too busy', but in reality because he feared the death he would have to encounter. He finally summoned the courage to attend, but he was too late and the man had already died. He said *I could not escape my irrational fear of death, which exposed the illusion that my role [as Minister] gave me control over death.* (Bottomley 2015:29)

After nine years in parish ministry, John found himself unemployed. After a short period working for a social research organisation and then completing a Graduate Diploma in Sociology from Latrobe University, John took a job as a research sociologist for the Union Shop Committee at Williamstown Naval Dockyards. The workingmen accepted John as a researcher and he learned to listen to the issues they raised about their workplace. It was here that he saw the world of work as a place of ministry and his research work as not simply a 'stop-gap' until another parish placement came up. Rather, it seemed to John that the world of work became his calling.

John was not the only minister is secular employment at that time in Victoria and he brought together a group of ministers who gathered in 1984, to offer their skills in the world of work as researchers and policy consultants. They formed the Urban Ministry Network (UMN) as an independent incorporated association. The Urban Ministry Network and the Centre for Creative Ministries (CCM) later merged to become the Creative Ministries Network (CMN), first as a stand-alone incorporated association and later as an agency of the Uniting Church. The Creative Ministries Network has now been renamed and subsumed into Uniting.

Originally, the group of ministers had tried to find a place within the Uniting Church and hoped to establish an urban ministry unit in Synod, but agreement on where such a unit would be placed and how it should be paid for led to UMN becoming an incorporated association. Interestingly, in 1996, the Urban Ministry Network was required to become an agency of UnitingCare under the Synod, because the Synod had no model constitution to fit the type of social justice work that UMN was doing. The only legal identity on offer was as a community service agency, even though this was not 'fit for purpose'. The same debate occurred again in 2015 when Uniting was created and, again, Creative Ministries Network did not fit the community service model, but found itself compelled to join.

The aim over the decades and through the variously named agencies was always to bring together worship and action in the world; the personal and the public spheres and the home and working lives of people John contacted, worked with and those to whom he offered support. John credits the support and solidarity of others in the community and its creativity and prayerfulness as the foundation for his later research and development of rituals for grief and bereavement.

Through the decade of the 1980s, the Urban Ministry Network undertook various funded research projects, including a study for the Occupational Health and Safety Commission on information for migrant workers, and the social impact on farmers of increasing land salinity. The Urban Ministry Network was instrumental in establishing the Church and Trade Unions Committee and the Victorian Injured Workers Centre, and commenced annual services of remembrance for work-related deaths and May Day (justice for workers).

In the decade of the 1990s, after John took on a part time ministry position with St George's, he began focusing on the creative arts as a way for people to find meaning in the story of their lives. He started the Centre for Creative Ministries. John believes that the gift of the arts as a means for embodying private truths in public truth-speaking may be a parable for the path by which Christ's transforming spirit may be embodied to address the grief and trauma at large in the world. By way of example, John received a grant to employ a writing tutor to help

Vietnam veterans explore and express their story. It resulted in one veteran and his wife preparing a book called *From Geelong To Nui Dat,* transforming their private grief into a public lament for the suffering of Vietnam veterans.

The Koori art program for Aboriginal women undertaking alcohol and drug rehabilitation at a local centre was also started around this time, developing from a CCM travelling art and music show for Aboriginal communities called "The Urban Dreaming Project". Art therapy workshops for wives bereaved by a work-related death commenced as a way of expressing and sharing grief.

Throughout the 1990s, the Urban Ministry Network was involved in work-related grief issues and in 1997, commenced its ministry with families bereaved by work-related deaths, and John also began providing pastoral supervision to clergy. In John's career, these were the first direct service activities in grief support that were funded. Field placements for theological and social work students began at UMN and CCM at this time, along with teaching in an Urban Ministry program at the United Faculty of Theology.

By 2003, the Boards of both entities (Urban Ministry Network and the Centre for Creative Ministries) came together under the governance policies of UnitingCare and, in 2004, the Creative Ministries Network was formed as a UnitingCare agency. Strangely, Uniting Church Synod governance policies for community service agencies refer neither to God, nor worship, nor the role and place of theological reflection. The new CMN Board took it upon itself to correct this omission and began to develop agency policies according to the Uniting Church governance manual, but with the inclusion of the Board's own theological reflection on issues. This book highlights the governance work of the Creative Ministries Network to embody both Word and deed. John called this process of governance development 'faith's wisdom and social science knowledge' to suggest what the agency sought to embody.

In the decade from 2004-2014, as Director of the Creative Ministries Network, John became increasingly involved in creative ways to be in solidarity with suffering people. In 2004, he established a monthly contemplative worship service, worked with Vietnam war veterans, developed songs of peace, created a Koori art program and even commissioned and developed a stage play called *Prophet and Loss*, which considered the writings of the prophet Isaiah in a modern-day setting. He also began researching the concept of restorative justice at this time.

John's interest in peace and reconciliation took on new dimensions when he met Bishop Daniel Thiagarajah from the Jaffna Diocese of the Church of South India when the Bishop visited Melbourne in 2007. John supported and encouraged the minister who followed him at St George's Church – Rev. Angela Tampiyappa – to actively pursue her long-held commitment to helping the Tamil people in northern Sri Lanka by entering into a partnership with CMN to raise funds for diocesan orphanages and pastors. The Bishop invited John to visit Jaffna in 2008 just after the cessation of Civil War hostilities – this visit started a long friendship and continuing collaboration. With the help of the Tamil diaspora community, St Georges and the CMN raised thousands of dollars for the Diocese.

John retired from the position of CEO of Creative Ministries Network in 2014. In 2015, John and Margaret travelled to Jaffna and lived in the community for six months, providing administrative, planning, training and pastoral support for the many programs that the Bishop and his wife had established to assist and empower impoverished local people struggling to recover from the injuries and deprivations of the civil war.

In 2016 CMN was merged with 23 other Uniting Church agencies and programs to form Uniting, the new body for all Victorian and Tasmanian Uniting Church community services agencies. Even after retirement, John still writes and engages in action for the disenfranchised. He calls his new consultancy Transforming Work and he writes and consults on making workplaces more just.

John has become closely involved with the work of Bishop Thiagrajah in Sri Lanka and co-authored a book with the Bishop that was published in 2016 for the tenth anniversary of the Bishop's consecration. John and Margaret keep in regular communication with friends and colleagues in Jaffna, return each year for a period of one month to continue this work; and the CMN congregation continues to provide some financial support for the Diocese. The "Sri Lanka Project" was an eye-opener for many, and gifted a more global perspective to the Creative Ministries Network.

The following chapters of this book outline the key fields of endeavour for John Bottomley, the Creative Ministries Network and its two predecessor agencies, the Urban Ministry Network and the Centre for Creative Ministries, bringing together in one place, the broad research areas, the key themes, teachings and practices from John's work and that of the agencies he either founded or worked for and of his colleagues over a 40-year period. As Appendix 2 shows in the titles and authors of the many reports over forty years, John gathered a large group of practitioners, ministers, supporters, researchers around the themes of the work.

Reflections on the Material in this Chapter

This Chapter summarises the working life of Revd John Bottomley. It notes his sense of calling to the life of a minister of religion and how his calling expanded to embrace being a researcher and consultant to the workplace and to workers.

- What do you notice most about John's working life?
- Have you ever experienced of a sense of 'calling'? How did it manifest itself? Did you listen?
- What contribution do you make to your community?
- Have you experienced a sense of frustration or a lack of purpose at work?
- Have you felt as if you just 'don't fit in' at work? Or that you want the organisation to go in a different direction?
- Have you ever worked with a colleague or leader who has influenced your direction?
- Have you been an inspiration to others?
- Have you experienced a big change of direction in your work life? Did you find it more satisfying to accept the change? Or did you struggle with the change? Perhaps it was forced upon you (by retrenchment, change in family circumstances, ill health). Or perhaps it came as a surprise.

CHAPTER 2

A CONSISTENT THREAD

If our church is not marked by caring for the poor, the oppressed, the hungry, we are guilty of heresy. Ignatius of Loyola[2]

This chapter notes the consistent thread in all of John's work that God calls us to be present in the world and to act to foster justice. Since John's writings traverse history, politics, philosophy and theology, this chapter offers a basic insight into the history of philosophy and ideas that centre on what it means to be human and to have lived a good and just life.

In this chapter, I summarise the thinking of many theorists and philosophers who have written about what it means to be human and to have lived a good life. I chose them as they have been the basis of the many talks John and I have had over the years. While he uses stories and wisdom from the Bible, from sociologists and from his experience to delve into the large question of the purpose of life, I offer my knowledge of political thinkers, philosophers and psychoanalysts. But, interestingly, we generally agree on big issues, although we use a different form of expression. Here, I try to recreate some of the flavour of our discussions to help the reader locate their own view on the 'meaning of life'.

> This chapter notes the consistent thread in all of John's work that God calls us to be present in the world and to act to increase justice

2   http://www.azquotes.com/quote/685993

After completing his Bachelor of Arts (Sociology) and theological studies, John Bottomley started his ordained ministry as a Methodist (and later Uniting Church) parish minister in 1974. After nearly a decade of service to the Church, he embarked on a different journey. John moved to a social research and consulting field of endeavour and the issues he covered, the reports he created or co-created, the topics he investigated were wide ranging. This section will outline those fields of endeavour and the serendipitous way they have become integrated over a life's work.

Across all John's work over forty years, there is a consistent thread and a recurring theme that unites the work. He seeks to explore what it means to be human. He doesn't offer answers for how to live; rather, he seeks to uncover the complexity of living. His writing stands in opposition to the powers he believes seek to control, subjugate and minimise the creativity of humankind and he writes in solidarity with the poor, the oppressed and the disenfranchised.

The body of work as a whole covers creative writing projects with Vietnam war veterans, contemplative worship, poetry, drama, liturgy, healing through story and song and healing through art – these are in addition to more traditional research reports that cover issues as varied as work and suicide, Aboriginal leadership in the Uniting Church, broadening participation in Technical and Further Education (TAFE), rituals and ceremonies for death, the social impact of salinity in farming areas, training materials for the legal fraternity, spiritual care needs of people with a disability, studies of church ministers and leaders in lay work, fair pay for shopping centre cleaners and workplace safety. A list of all reports authored by John and/or colleagues (including myself) are noted at Appendix 2.

Whilst being a consultant and social researcher 'for hire', John worked in collaboration with others and tried to combine his sense of faith with the work in every project he took on. From early on, he was clear that the Word of God should not be separated from the deeds or activities we carry out. The Word comes first in his belief and should guide all actions subsequently. For John, God wants each of us to live a fully human life and God provides the means for us to do this. John believes that God requires that we act justly and work towards improving justice for everyone. Belief in God is insufficient, without this action. *And what does the Lord require of you? To act justly and to love mercy and to walk humbly with your God* (Micah 6:8). John saw that there was inequality in the world and that workplaces are sites of that inequality. Further, he understood in the stories he heard from the disenfranchised that suffering is partly caused by the limited way most of us tend to live these days – with family and home life separated from professional and work life.

> This book uses the insights gained over John Bottomley's full working life to help readers to think for themselves about the big questions of life and to reflect if they are on the right path for themselves. What does it mean to be a whole person in the late 20th and early 21st centuries? How can we have the freedom to live a fully human life and also learn from the struggle to conform to the constraints of the society we inhabit?

John writes about the difference between merely working to survive in the world and being *called* to make a difference to the world. John's view is that we are all called to make the world a better place, but that sometimes we do not hear the call because we 'forget' our lives are a gift of the Creator. My view is that the culture of our day is dominated by corporate capitalism, which imposes a sense of competition for scarce resources on everything we do. It makes us feel as if life comprises winners and losers and if we are to survive, we must win at any cost. The prevailing culture can drown out any call for us to work to bring about justice and foster the wellbeing of others. John's view, threaded through his work, is that the church too is captured by this prevailing view.

As I noted in my Introduction, I met John in 1984 and we have worked on projects together and had many interesting discussions over the decades encompassing these large questions relating to what it means to live a meaningful and purposeful life. A helpful example of how we both think and work together is described in a paper we wrote together and which we called *Has God Stopped Calling?* (Dempsey & Bottomley 2011).Our published paper demonstrates the capture of the church. I will refer to it by way of illustration of this major theme in John's work and the way we have discussed issues from our two perspectives.

Has God Stopped Calling or Has the Church Stopped Listening?

Has God Stopped Calling reminds the reader of the fundamental tenet of the institutional church that some people are called by God to become Ministers of Religion and following this call, it is then the church's task and duty to prepare them for the role. Religious service is a vocation where a person is moved to serve on the basis of a personal sense that God has called them to this service. But after saying this, we note that a particular church report that we analyse seems to contradict this fundamental premise.

The church report that we analyse outlines – by way of data tables, graphs and charts – how both lay people attending church services and the numbers called to ordained ministry have been falling steadily over the past fifteen to twenty years. The key message of the report is that the church is both 'shrinking and aging' and that, therefore, a marketing intervention is required. The report then suggests that church members must be more proactive, seeking out people who are suitable for ordination and then asking them to come forward for ordination. The church is urged not to wait for candidates to present themselves, but to actively seek out those whom church members consider to have 'gifts' and encourage them to dedicate their lives to service in the church. The Uniting Church report urges the church to take an active role in 'tapping potential candidates on the shoulder'.

This suggests that the church in its current institutional form is given priority over waiting for God to call. The report we examined then lists a set of strategic actions to create the circumstances for people to come forward for ordination. Essentially, these involve a committee that would oversee the work of a full time paid project officer to implement the planned initiatives. Thus the idea of ordained ministry as a vocation seems to have been lost, as has been the concept of vocation in business today (Sennett 1998). The church report suggests that the church needs to take the initiative in calling people to service and should no longer wait for God to do so.

We began the discussion that led to this published paper with John expressing his frustration that the institutional church was blind to its capture by business language and business solutions for what is a spiritual question. Whereas I came to the issue thinking, the church report betrays a deep fear of organisational death or irrelevance. I sensed a collective panic over loss of purpose and a clutching at straws to save the institution in its present form. John asked where was the quiet, thoughtful reflection on what God's purpose might be for the church in our times. I said why would a church employ a marketing plan to have more Ordained Ministers? We both agreed that there was deeper anxiety in the church about its possible abandonment by God.

Our analysis was critical of the Uniting Church for using the discourse of business and seeking to employ management tools and techniques to halt a decline in the number of people presenting with a calling to be Ordained Ministers. Our view was that this significant issue of decline in the church was tackled in a narrowly defined and secular way. The need of the church to 'stay alive' in its present form was given priority over reflection, prayer and discernment of the meaning behind fewer people apparently being called by God.

From my perspective, the desire to be active in seeking a simple solution (the marketing strategy) is a sign of an institution's avoidance of the fear and anxiety about its own impending demise and I often see this in my consulting work where organisations are frantically busy to avoid a perceived threat of destruction. The illusion of rationality is maintained by appealing to business solutions for a problem that is essentially about the fear of the death of the organisation. For John, taking the task of ensuring more people come forward to be ordained into its own hands demonstrates how far the church has strayed from its own beliefs and how much it is captured by the secular discourse of business in our time. If it is God's will to choose people for a calling, then what makes the church think it can take matters of God into its own hands?

We both agreed that Ordained Ministry is a particular historically and socially constructed form of religious service and that it is neither essential nor inevitable for this to be the form of church in the future. We also agreed that the world of work is the place where the church should be most active and yet it is not. By using a business model and a marketing strategy to take over God's role in calling those to a religious vocation, the church has succumbed to the prevailing secular view of business, economy and the market as the primary mode of connection between humanity.

Both John and I think of the primacy of business language and business tools and techniques and their unthinking application in all spheres as *hegemony*. In other words, they are the dominant way of speaking and we rarely question their applicability to faith-based organisations. Paradoxically, the church report we critique uses the language of this hegemony to defend its parochial, 19th century view of what church 'should' look like and still avoids the world of work, where it is most sorely needed.

When the business model is adopted as the best model for all human activity and all other ways of organising ourselves are criticised as inferior or simply wrong, then we are caught in the prevailing cultural view and fantasy assumptions about what life means. I see this often in my work as a consultant to business – the client wants a quick, simple solution to a complex problem. I am often asked to implement a strategy or introduce values into a business or organisation, where the reasons for lack of success are assumed to be rational and easily fixed. I am sometimes asked to implement strategies to make staff work harder, be more efficient, focus on their task, work as a team, give one hundred percent, live the company values and so forth.

What I see, though, when I enter these workplaces (as a consultant) is the pain, sadness and suffering of staff who struggle each day to find a purpose in their busyness and who wish the organisation cared for them as people. They seek trust, support, understanding, but instead they get KPIs (key performance indicators), risk aversion, audit and output requirements. I am sometimes asked to "fix" an underperforming team, as if the team were a machine that just needs some fine-tuning, instead of understanding the deeply human and non-rational motivations of the team.

People bring their whole selves to work, and the rational language of business cannot fix every complex problem associated with people and their relationships. What happens in business is too often put forward as a good model for all spheres of human activity (Du Gay 2000). For me, this is too narrow a focus to truly solve our human problems and, for John, this is not what God wants for us.

The church report John and I analysed paradoxically ignores the world of work and the calling of church members to their service of God in industry and commerce, and then borrows almost exclusively from these spheres to shape its strategies for the Church's salvation. This is a strange reversal of the history of 'call' in the Church. From the medieval period, God's call was confined to people called to priesthood or religious orders. Then from the Reformation, God's call became associated with every possible form of human service, from the milkmaid, to judge, to husband/wife and citizen. The report appears to have ignored the richness of the early Protestant insight into 'the priesthood of all believers' and the complexity of engagement with industry and commerce. The church's report has withdrawn into a simpler medieval pattern which recapitulates the dualism between church and world. It seems the institutional church will do anything to stay in existence, in its present form, but cannot seem to ask whether a new form is required.

This is why, at the beginning of this book, I use the quote from the Old Testament prophet, Amos, who tells Israel that God is not interested in religious offerings, songs and services (worse, God hates it), if the people do not then go out into the world and ensure that justice prevails. It seems to me that this is the calling to believers, to act in the world to create a world that is righteous and just. This is the calling and the meaning of living a 'good and worthy' life: for every person to do whatever we are called to do in order to make the world a just place. I think John would argue from a theological standpoint that God has placed the human self in community from the beginning. As the theologian, Brueggemann (2015:86) says

> *the self is a member of community and never an isolated or self-sufficient entity. As both vulnerable and powerful, the human self lives in a drama between life and death, strength and weakness. The human self waxes and wanes as the gifts of life are given or withheld, received or resisted. The self is mortal and finite...and death is the edge of human existence, all the rest is left to the rule of God.*

What does it mean to live a fully human life?

So, if God is no longer calling Ministers of Religion to the local parish and the idea of a calling or vocation is falling into disuse and people are using the language of business to define all sorts of social issues, what can it mean in the 21st century to have lived a 'good life'?

John's work considers this question from many angles. He uses sociological perspectives, theological and scriptural insights and an historically critical viewpoint to try to get to the heart of what it means to live well, respond to a call or vocation and how to increase justice in the world. But before we can summarise and learn from John's working life, it will be helpful to explore the wisdom from past thinkers who also tried to explain how to live well. To understand the lessons from John's work, we must begin to consider what it means to be fully human and to live a good life, and I will do this by briefly looking at what philosophers and political thinkers have told us. For John's work compares and contrasts the thinking of the Enlightenment period and that of the period of modernity that followed it. John uses the thinking of theologians and philosophers to untangle the mysteries. For me, the period following the Enlightenment is the period of industrialisation and the rise of capitalism as the main force in politics and economics. What follows is a simple summary of thinking about the purpose and value of human life over the centuries, provided in order to set the scene for a discussion of the key themes of John's work in chapter four.

Philosophers and ethicists throughout history have considered the value and purpose of humanity, both individually and in society: the self in isolation and in community. Much of western thought derives from the teachings of Socrates, Plato and Aristotle in ancient Greek times. The ancient Greek philosophers, in particular, concerned themselves with defining what is means to have lived a good life. Socrates famously tells us that the unexamined life is not worth living. He was well known for asking difficult questions that embarrassed and humiliated those in power.

One of Socrates' students was Plato, who argued in his writing that there exists the imperfect physical world and there also exists the soul of humans that seeks the higher order of perfection in beauty, goodness, justice, courage, but which is bound by the reality of existence. Plato wrote in dialogue form, in other words he did not proclaim what was right or correct, but he rather debated all aspects of a problem in his writings.

John's writing has themes in common with both Socrates and Plato. He asks the hard questions and examines an issue from many angles to open it up to investigation. The most famous student of Plato was Aristotle, who rejected Plato's concept of the forms (beauty, justice and so on) as a reality to strive for and instead argued that logic and reason are the key to understanding the natural world. Aristotle is the key philosopher who influenced the material view of the world: what we can see and touch is all that exists and the goal of life is happiness in his view. The way to achieve happiness is by engaging in virtuous actions over a lifetime.

In medieval times, most key thinkers and philosophers were religious believers and their questions were religious in nature. St Augustine wrote on the nature of humankind as having a body and soul, with the soul being the superior form. Later St Thomas Aquinas wrote commentaries on Aristotle's work in attempts to marry it with religious belief. He argued for the logic and reason of the material world as Aristotle did, but he also believed that wisdom and truth could only be achieved through divine intervention. He argued that reason and faith are compatible and co-operative as both scientific knowledge and faith come from God and things that exist are of themselves good, since God created them. Interestingly, St Thomas Aquinas tried to see a harmony and balance between the apparent opposites of reason and faith: he argued that without divine revelation, discoveries were not made and that careful reasoning could improve our understanding of faith.

Two things to note up to this point: philosophers had most often talked of humankind as individuals and not in relationship with each other or the earth, and they also considered reason and faith as opposites. This distinction can still be seen today. John takes a theological stance, which does not pit faith against reason, but rather considers faith as, perhaps, another word for trust. The faithful person has trust that God's Word is true and while we are faithful to it, then abundance will follow. I note that 'faith' nowadays tends to connote a private and personal belief in something which cannot be proved and is therefore of little value.

Aquinas was one of the early medieval philosophers who considered humankind in social contexts. He believed in natural law, which governs right and wrong and where we use our reason to act properly, but that we need the virtues to achieve it (particularly faith, hope and charity). Aquinas argued that there are three kinds of law: state law, which is the law that we abide by in society and which ought to grow from natural law (which is the rational means by which we all are guided in our nature towards the good) and finally there is eternal law, which could be roughly summed up as the divinely inspired order of everything. The earth is made and cared for by God and therefore it is good.

The contrast I notice in John's writing is the centrality of relationship - with God first, and with others, to having lived a 'good' life. It is interesting that across western philosophy, the focus on relationship seems limited. The philosophers I am briefly summarising here seem more concerned with reasoning our way to living well. But I am certainly not doing justice to the whole history of philosophy, or theology, nor attempting to. I am merely introducing concepts to help position the reader for a discussion of John's views (and mine) as we progress.

Following the mediaeval period, philosophers began to move away from trying to reconcile reason and faith and looked more closely at the way society was structured, its inequalities and how we are governed. Philosopher Thomas Hobbs began thinking about the importance of relationship and suggested in *The Leviathan* in 1651 that without connection with others in community, we revert to a short, lonely, brutish life.

During the period of the Age of Reason (17th century) and the Enlightenment (18th century) there were advances in science, with a growth in understanding of how the human body and the natural world function. The times called for scientific and rational study of all things, with no reliance on God or religious belief to dictate what one should believe, but rather that fact, truth and evidence should determine belief. Age of Reason thinkers believed that humankind is 'perfectible', that is, we can and will improve ourselves over time as we uncover more scientific truth about the natural world and ourselves. It was a belief, really, in the positive forward trajectory of progress and human development and for our social lives. These thinkers held that our ability to reason is the key to our perfectibility (Goudzwaard 1979).

The privileging of reason and logic above faith and emotion continues today, as does the dualism inherent in this worldview. Reason, logic, evidence and fact became paramount and (in Kant's view) humanity was freed from having to believe what someone else tells us, to determining for ourselves what to believe and how to act, using our own intellectual abilities. It led to the notion that we are each masters of our own destiny and it is up to each of us to succeed in life by our own individual merits. For Nietzsche this meant the 'death of god' but also the rise of nihilism where nothing has absolute moral value and where humankind is adrift in a world of great freedom and potential, but lacking a set of values to guide us.

John Bottomley calls the Enlightenment period thinking - which postulates the pre-eminence of reason, humankind's perfectibility and dominance over nature - as an heroic, but doomed attempt to cheat death.

The belief system of modernity requires the commitment of autonomous human beings to their work to ensure the all-encompassing social goal of personal and social progress is carried forward. (Bottomley 2015:23)

In fact John goes further to suggest that the primacy of the individual, the mastery of life, the ideal of work as self-fulfilment have become ideology today. Ideology is a system of beliefs that is so pervasive that it goes unquestioned. These opinions are so all encompassing that they are invisible to us for what they truly are, which is, merely one way of thinking and viewing the world. When a view becomes ideology it is unavailable for critique. It becomes 'just the way things are'.

John and I enjoy discussing the centrality of relationship in life as opposed to the idea of the autonomous individual conquering all before him. For John, this is a view that discounts the primacy of God and for me it goes against what I know of psychology and in particular the Object-Relations School of psychotherapy.

I studied the psychoanalyst, Melanie Klein (1975) during my PhD. She observed infants in their play and noted the stages of maturity that they each go through. She noticed that the infant develops its view of the world only in relationship to other objects or people. At first the infant cannot account for differences between its own needs and the ability of another to satisfy them. The infant believes itself to be good and the other non-helpful person to be bad. The infant longs for the return of the good person who can 'fix' everything. Klein calls this 'splitting', whereby we are stuck in binary positions and see the other as all bad and the self as all good. She describes our adult human tendency to idealise and anathematise: to forcibly separate the 'all good' from the 'all bad' in life as a reversion to a very early form of thought present in infancy. She believes that we tend to replay these stages of relationships with self and others throughout life.

In this split, rigid and binary position, the other is an object, not a person like ourselves. We separate ourselves and our supposed innocence (Klein called this the fantasy of the pristine self) from the wicked and persecutory elements 'outside' of each of us that may want to hurt us. Growth and maturity, in the Kleinian view, comes with insight into the fact that we tend to put the blame on externalities (as we do in now in economics) and imagine a deliberate persecutory mindset of others to hurt each of us but that this is in fact all in our own mind! Maintaining this view, allows us to focus on ourselves as good, pure, happy and anything bad that occurs must therefore come from 'outside'.

These are very primitive self-object dyads and yet we can see them in political dialogue now (Trump building a wall to keep Mexicans out – they are all rapists and drug dealers), when the truth is, surely, that we each have the capacity for both good and bad behaviours and pretending we don't is immature. Obviously, these split ways of thinking fade as we grow and mature, but in times of fear and in regimes that encourage the split, we can see their echo. I see it when we call an unethical person at work, a 'bad apple', as if that person is separate, different and certainly not like us, who are always ethical. And I see it when the Uniting Church calls for a marketing solution in desperation that not enough ministers are being called by God.

The value of psychoanalytic theorists to a consideration of what it means to live a life of value (however defined) is that they all *agree that beneath the crust of techno-rational culture is a dark side rooted in unconscious processes and in early childhood experiences that profoundly affect later life* (Stein & Allcorn 2014:345). They argue that the surface appearance of humans as rational, objective, autonomous, technical and materialistic is just a thin crust, which belies the irrational and emotional life that goes on underneath the façade of rationality.

In theology, the self cannot be thought of without reference firstly to God and of course in philosophy and psychology the same view is not always shared. I am not meaning to critique theology, but rather I am commenting that in our conversations, John and I come from different starting points (theology as talk about God and psychoanalysis as attempts to understand the self) and that we often agree. Whether coming from a standpoint of theology or philosophy and psychoanalysis, John and I see that it is in love, connectedness and community that we see a more nuanced picture that there is both good and bad in ourselves, in complex situations and in other people. The view that we are each autonomous, self-interested and rational is a strongly held proposition that has held sway since the Enlightenment. In his work, John describes the time period following the Enlightenment as 'modernity' and he speaks of its trademark adherence to the notion of the primacy of a rational economic model of life.

The dominant economic system in western countries following the Enlightenment has been capitalism. The dominant discourse of the last thirty years in western countries is neoliberalism (sometimes called economic rationalism), which is an ideology arguing for the primacy and the 'correctness' of free market capitalism, whereby rational thought, scientific truth and economic and technological progress have almost a religious significance and ultimate status to determine what it means to live a fully human life. John said to me recently that the hegemony of modernity provides the cultural foundations for capitalism to exist, with belief in God now consigned to the private realm.

The ideology of modernity – is the heroic individuality of humankind to tame and control the environment in the pursuit of progress.

Capitalism is our current economic system in which goods are owned and traded by private individuals or businesses. The 'father' of modern capitalism, Adam Smith argued in 1776 in *The Wealth of Nations* that society functions best with the free and unencumbered circulation of money, goods and labour. The production and cost of goods and services is based on supply and demand in the market, with little intervention or planning by governments or powerful elites. It is from this treatise, originating nearly 250 years ago, that the basic tenets of today's neoliberal capitalism have grown. Smith argues that self-interest allows for the buying and selling of goods and services (for profit) around the globe.

Adam Smith did see a role for taxation and for government involvement in the economic market, but essentially he felt it worked most efficiently if it was free. We hear this sort of rhetoric in neoliberal thought today in terms such as the level playing field, the free market, free enterprise, self-regulating market, market economy, free trade (surely a thing of the past), open market and the like. It assumes that everyone is equal in both their buying and selling capacity and the cost of goods and services is set in the market by their level of demand (the desire to have the good or service) and their scarcity (things that are hard to find are worth more).

The UK is experiencing the complexities of removing itself from a market economy now with Brexit. The European Union describes itself as a single market with the free movement of goods, capital, services and labour within its boundaries[3] thereby using Smith's *own words* to describe itself two hundred and fifty years later.

Our capitalist societies function now because citizens accept this notion that free circulation of capital gives everyone

---

3   https://ec.europa.eu/growth/single-market_en

a chance at wealth. It seems implicitly believed that a good life is equal to a wealthy life because wealth brings happiness. Therefore we each need to work hard to achieve success and a high price can, of course, be put on goods and services that are in scarce supply and high demand. The primacy of the market and economic thinking, which dates back to Smith, have become the dominant way of viewing society and have replaced religious faith (in my view) as the pre-eminent worldview within capitalist economies. We accept as the prevailing truth that we are free and can each succeed with equal opportunity to do so. We believe that happiness and having lived a good life is mostly about individual success and the accumulation of material wealth. We also believe (as if it were an article of faith) that reason and logic make us superior to animals and that belief in God is a private matter and has no bearing on the way the world works.

Antonio Gramsci (1891-1937) called this cultural hegemony. By this he means that the ruling class in a capitalist society maintains power by proposing and promoting its own values and norms as if they were perfectly normal, common sense, the only way to think or organise ourselves. While Karl Marx suggested capitalism would be overthrown when workers rose up and seized control over the market, later Gramsci saw a more insidious manipulation going on in capitalist regimes. He thought that institutions, deliberately and with sinister intent, promote the idea that we are all individuals working hard for our individually prosperous futures and everyone is equal. This idea is so pervasive that everyone begins to believe it to be self-evident.

While we should surely do no harm, this view implies it is not an individual's responsibility to serve others or to contribute to the greater good – rather, we should each look after ourselves first. Perhaps we simply have to work hard to be successful and happy and count our life as worthwhile? At the end of our life, each of us can look back knowing we lived a good life by seeing our material wealth, how far up the ladder of workplace success we climbed, or our own family's health.

Capitalist ideology has expanded to become the dominant way of thinking today not just in the economic market place, but in every aspect of life. Today, everything has become a product to be bought and sold; people are 'customers' first and foremost, every individual is responsible for their own success or failure (Verhaege 2012). The value of a life is commodified in the same way. Former British Prime Minister Margaret Thatcher is famous for arguing that there are only individuals working hard for themselves ...*there is no such thing as society: there are individual men and women, and there are families.* But John asks: is this how things must be? Is this how God wants it to be?

In a speech at the University of Kansas in1968, Robert Kennedy[4] lucidly explained the vacuous nature of considering that everything is for buying or selling and everything has a price on it.

Yet the gross national product does not allow for the health of our children, the quality of their education or the joy of their play. It does not include the beauty of our poetry or the strength of our marriages, the intelligence of our public debate or the integrity of our public officials. It measures neither our wit nor our courage, neither our wisdom nor our learning, neither our compassion nor our devotion to our country, it measures everything in short, except that which makes life worthwhile.

4   https:/jfklibrary.org/Research/Research-Aids/Ready-Reference/RFK-Speeches/Remarks-of-Robert-F-Kennedy-at-the-University-of-Kansas-March-18-1968.aspx

And back in the 18th century, the 'father of modern capitalism', Adam Smith also wrote *The Theory of Moral Sentiments* where he claims humanity has a natural affinity for the virtue of sympathy for the plight of others. Yet, we hardly hear of this volume by Smith. He did not foresee progress as 'economic man' without a concurrent moral progress associated with lasting social values. Smith argued that humans are both self-interested – and it is prudent to be so – but also endowed with a natural sympathy (we might say empathy today) for the plight of our fellows. We do feel their pain and suffering and we can place ourselves (more or less) in the shoes of the other. How strange it is that one of the books of Adam Smith has become a "bible" today, but the other is forgotten. Smith argued both for the 'wealth of nations' and that this must not occur without 'moral sentiments'. These days, while business 'nods' to the idea of values, these are largely window dressing and are in reality quite separate from business and handed over to the clergy for Sunday service.

The question of how to live well while doing as we each please and also living in harmony with others is a complex conundrum. If self-interest is prudent, as Smith advises, how do we also live in harmony with and help others around us? When should we focus on ourselves first? When do we care for others? Philosophers have either tended to see humanity as inherently good and our societies as ways to organise ourselves in order to improve how we support each other, or, that we are inherently selfish and we make an agreement (a social contract) to live together in society where laws exist to curb our excesses.

Freud took a more personal angle and famously suggests (in *Civilisation and its Discontents* 1930: 262) *[T]he question of the purpose of human life has been raised countless times; it has never yet received a satisfactory answer and perhaps does not admit of one.* Freud saw the role of society as having a civilising influence on the greedy and aggressive nature of humankind. But Adam Smith saw that moderation needs to be in place so that our natural tendency to want to care for others, especially the weak and vulnerable, can be exercised as well as our desire for self-accumulation.

The idea that we may be either naturally selfish or naturally unselfish has been debated in philosophy both in religious medieval times as well as during the post religious periods of the Enlightenment and modernity. God created us as good beings, but we fell from grace in the Adam and Eve story, and in Adam Smith's view, we naturally and obviously must care for ourselves first before we can care for others. The arguments for our nature as either good or bad, for life being short and brutish or filled with care and concern for others, has tended to be seen in rather narrow and binary terms - as either one or the other. A good life is either a successful and selfish one for us individually or it is a life of sacrifice for others.

My view is that this binary way of looking at life is narrow and unhelpful because Enlightenment thinkers relegated the binary opposites of fact as they saw it (emotion, creativity, belief in God, care of others) to the private sphere of people's lives. They imagined emotional experience and expression to be in opposition to rational thought; belief in divine providence is imagined to be in opposition to scientific truth; and human wellbeing is imagined to be in opposition (or at least subservient) to economic and technological progress.

The theory of the social contract whose purpose is to keep all of humanity 'in line' within a society was popular for centuries until Hegel pondered the dialectic nature of dualisms of the past (mind and body, self and other, freedom and authority, reason and faith) and Marx considered the corrosive impact of power in society and its unequal impacts on its own members. Hegel was dismissive of binaries and overly simplistic arguments that meant one view is right and another is wrong. He argued that new things are discovered directly from the debate of opposing views – knowledge and improvement in any sphere can be gained only by the 'to and fro' of ideas. It is in the connectedness and the dialogue to uncover connectedness that new ways of being emerge. We might call this 'bouncing ideas off one another' and it was a way to see the synthesis and connectedness of all things, rather than the rightness of one argument and the subsequent exclusion of the opposing view. It is similar in essence to the iterative way that John Bottomley deals with complex issues. He listens and hears from those who are being harmed, learns, discusses, studies and reflects and finally develops a theological perspective.

Human nature – complex and contested

The key to these philosophical debates over the centuries is the complexity and contested nature of our humanity. We all want to connect with others, be safe, prosper, form bonds of trust and love and at the same time be free to do as we please. The Hegelian dialectic – the view of the interrelatedness of the natural world and humankind – is noted here because it describes the way that conclusions are arrived at in the work of John Bottomley. It is this complexity, connectedness and conflictedness of life, which is examined in John's work. Rather than thinking of humankind as selfish or selfless, "all good" or "all bad", John investigates the mystery that we are both good and bad and that we strive both individually and also as social creatures to live a good life (however we may define it).

The binary view (seeing only either/or) is not helpful and not in keeping with a true exploration of what life means. It is an extension of logic and reason so admired in the Enlightenment period and our modern era to argue that if one thing is right, then all other propositions must be wrong. This hyper rationality hides a more primitive binary that shapes us from early life. It is only with experience and maturity that we can learn that one truth does not necessarily negate another and that how we live and thrive, changes and adapts as we interact socially. As Sutton (2017) says, neuroscience has now demonstrated that...*we are in fact social animals, in continual emotional and neurobiological call and response with the people around us, whether we know it or not.*

From a theological perspective, John sees redemption in brokenness and grace arising from acknowledgment of failure; from a sociological perspective, he sees that organisational and political structures limit each of us in our search for our own fulfilment, and they can also hinder our ability to support and help others. Further, from a career of working with those who do not fit the model of the successful corporate citizen, he has seen and understood the pain inflicted by exclusion and marginalisation.

We are all, of course, complex and contradictory and this is both the challenge and task of life to stay with this exploration and see the possibilities it allows. This is the Hegelian dialectic applied to relationships, rather than ideas. In order to love and be loving, we need to work at integrating both love and hate of ourselves and of others. It is the integration that brings about a new creative response to the world and an ability to cope with ambiguity. John would say that by seeing our own failings and seeking forgiveness of God, we can enter a state of grace, where we can be made whole, despite, perhaps, not deserving it! Thinking that we each are 'all good' and the other is 'all bad' leads– in John's view – to us being out of right relationship with God and therefore with others. In that state of isolation and self-righteousness, we may feel independent and in control, but we cannot creatively work with others to build justice.

The idea of the autonomous individual forging his/her own path towards success is a myth that capitalism has given us and it is hegemonic –it is socially, politically, economically and culturally dominant in our lives today. The heroic individual is so pervasive an idea that we seem incapable of believing it is not so. A Uniting Church minister once told me that capitalism is the best economic system we have so far. For me, this is a staggering view from a minister of religion. Is capitalism really the system that Jesus would prefer to see - where profit is made by companies and individuals at the expense of others in our communities? Where health care, gaols, detention centres, nursing homes, childcare are not services for citizens, but rather profit-making enterprises? If I recall my Bible studies correctly, Jesus went into the Temple and threw out the people buying and selling there, calling them thieves. We live in societies now where everything including human labour is a product to be bought or sold and where everyone must survive in this cut-throat world by their own success or failure. We have absorbed the idea that *my* success can only be bought by *your* failure.

But the eminent physicist, Einstein (1950/2005:206) said:

A human being is part of the whole, called by us, "Universe", a part limited in time and space. He experiences himself, his thoughts and feelings as something separate from the rest, a kind of optical delusion of his consciousness.

John's work discusses from many angles what constitutes having lived a good life and he uncovers and questions the ideology that 'working hard will lead to success'. He sees the dominance of this view as hegemony. He argues that we do not see its dominance, we do not see its hold on us and we do not see the danger of it. We simply believe it is the only way we can live and organise ourselves in society today. But John says *the promise of industrialised society that hard work brings its own reward is a lie* (Bottomley 2015:39).

The defining characteristic of our current epoch is that it is both wonderful and dreadful (Berman 1982). Most nations on this earth are at their most prosperous time in recorded history. We have advances in science and medicine that were not dreamt of in past times; we have technology that unites us and makes all people on earth closer than at any time past. We have seen spectacular economic growth accompanied by lower mortality rates, improved population health and the eradication of disease. But we also have tremendous waste occurring at the same time, with devastation of the natural world occurring at rates faster than we can find solutions. Wars continue to be waged and across many nations there are millions who do not 'gather at the feast' offered by the discoveries of our modern existence and our systems of distributing life's essentials.

In modern times, Richard Sennett (1998) has written extensively on the breaking down of social bonds that is caused by the individual mindset where everything is a commodity to be bought and sold. In *Corrosion of Character*, he examines the fact that many of us are materially better off than our parents or grandparents, but at a cost. Sennett's thesis is that the short term, contractual nature of the modern workplace undermines the values of trust, loyalty, commitment and obligation to others. He believes the flexibility of the modern workplace is in fact a new form of oppression. This increase in workplace flexibility may appear to give greater freedom and unprecedented development opportunities, but it can also cause feelings of insecurity and disorientation, which are experienced as loss. This is exactly what John has also found in his studies.

Sennett argues that the lack of continuity and narrative of one's life work gives rise to disconnection and loss. In *The Craftsman* (2009) he talks about the opportunity offered by the making of something to think about the greater good as we engage in creating from start to finish. He speaks of the release of creativity resulting from actually making something and the skill of living with ambiguity as a new task is mastered or a new item shaped.

In a similar way, labour was its own reward in the distant past. But in capitalism, the physical strength, creativity or the intellectual work of individuals is bought and sold in a manner separate to the creation of a finished product for the use and enjoyment of the person who made it. Our labour is a commodity and is no longer indistinguishable from our intrinsic humanity. This idea of creativity being expressed through the continuity of relationship is also apparent in John's work. He finds that those who suffer injustice are energised by opportunities and projects that give them a creative outlet – to paint, photograph, tell or write a story.

In some ways, Richard Sennett is a similar writer to John Bottomley: he has a good grasp of historical matters and ranges across philosophy and sociology when promoting his views. He also tries to see the complexity in a given topic and avoids the "black and white" view of the world. In all of John's work and that of the organisations he worked for, he has similarly tried to grapple with the Hegelian dialectic as a fundamental issue, both in how he undertook the paid work that was offered and in the writing of reports and research undertaken. Many of the reports contend with offering recommendations in order to facilitate change, while also telling the story of those who have suffered at the hands of the body seeking those recommendations. He also tried to model this complexity in the way he led the organisations he was involved in.

While Aristotle's logic was concerned with separate, discrete elements and discovering truth by moving from general principles that are already known to be true down to a specific conclusion (which excludes other viewpoints in a deductive manner), Hegel dissolves this rather static view by considering the gaining of knowledge as a dynamic movement towards the whole. In Hegel's philosophy, the whole is an overcoming[5] which preserves what it overcomes. When both an idea and its opposite come together, new knowledge is formed, which is both transformed, but which encompasses elements of the previous. In this sense, history is honoured and not forgotten.

In Hegelian terms, the struggle that John often faced has been how to write a report that is required by the funder of the research, but which also allows the voices of the voiceless to be heard and the true complexity of every situation to be uncovered in the work. There are no easy answers or simple solutions. Pain, injustice, fear and failure are important elements in a story that aims to tell the truth. Sometimes we don't want to hear the pain in another's story, as it is too close to our own. But being truly heard is a gift that workers in Uniting can offer their clients.

Speaking for others

A social researcher often speaks on behalf of those who have no voice. This position raises ethical questions: how do I best represent the key message from the people who have shared their story with me? As John's career progressed, he moved away from speaking *for* those he researched, towards speaking

---

5   Hegel used the term *Aufhebung*, which is most often translated to mean sublation. But Aufhebung is a curious word that can mean to lift up, or to suspend or even to abolish, transcend or preserve.

through their stories and issues to finally, allowing them to *speak for themselves* in his work. As a part of this career of writing, John began to become clearer regarding the connections between the specific issue he may be researching at a given time and the yearning for wholeness that he saw both in himself and in the participants of his research. He began to see the binaries and opposites that we construct for ourselves and the pain and suffering that they inflict upon all of us, but most particularly on those who are hurt or disenfranchised.

As previously mentioned, John's writing career culminated in his book, *Hard Work Never Killed Anybody*, in which he draws upon insights gained from listening and writing the stories of those who are broken and marginalised, to examine what it means to be human. He counters the simplistic notion that hard work can make each of us whole and fulfilled and the splitting he sees between work and family, private and public, morality and economics, which allow this 'deadly lie' to take hold and be the new religion of the modern world.

When reviewing his work over time, I observed that, initially, John tried to speak for the voiceless and to have the voices of power (usually government or employers) recognise the damage done in their name to the poor and disenfranchised. He tried to 'translate' the lived experience of those he interviewed or researched into the language of policy and the language of the law, so that things might change for the better. Later, he developed more creative ways to bring the message forward. He explored poetry, song, plays and artwork and through these ventures, found that creative outlets improve the wellbeing of those who suffer injustice and help them to give voice to their pain in ways that invite the viewer and listener to enter their world. Later still, he offered peer support activities to injured workers and to families bereaved by the death of a loved one at work. This work led to a companioning model of service, whereby the supported person is the one who leads the support; the client (as described in typical professional support programs) being the one who guides the style, substance, duration and direction of the support. The companioning model will be discussed in detail in the next chapter.

In summary, I wish to draw two key points from John's career of written work. John writes about the separation of the private and the public spheres in today's modern society, the breakdown in relationship between humankind as a result of this split, leading to injustice and suffering and he comments on the mirroring of that split in the church which separates mission from worship. Much of the quiet reflection in John's many reports and writings grapple with the limitations of a rational and often binary view of human life, with a belief in linear notion of inevitable progress at its core.

As a minister of religion, John believes that God must be placed first in order to truly understand what it means to be human and to have lived a good life. Psalm 139 sums it up thus: -

For it was you who formed my inward parts;
You knit me together in my mother's womb.
I praise you, for I am fearfully and wonderfully made.

This chapter has given the reader a rather rudimentary summary of the history of philosophical thought in order to prepare us for looking at the breadth of John Bottomley's work in the next chapter. In it, I detail the phases of John's career and the types of reports he wrote; the art, poetry, plays that were staged and the lessons he learnt from participating in a life of research and service.

Reflections on the material in this chapter

This chapter has briefly summarised philosophical thinking that tries to explain over the centuries how people can live a good life, both individually but also in care for others. I noted that as religious belief fell out of favour (in the Enlightenment period) and rational, logical thought processes came to the fore, these helped us to uncover the laws governing the function of the natural world. But this materialistic thinking also shaped the dominant economic view of the world that currently holds us today, i.e. that humankind is selfish and that it is natural to be so and that a price can be put on any item, good and service on earth, especially if it is scarce and hard to obtain: that life is measured by how hard we work and those who work hard will be rewarded. Melanie Klein's work explores possible origins for our developing moral compass and the real complexities of navigating our complex social relationships. This chapter also notes the Hegelian view that the truth can be discovered by an inductive and speculative form of thinking, where the whole is seen from a merging of 'both/and', rather than 'either/ or' and that John's work takes this dialectic view of the way to find truth.

- Have you ever thought about these 'big' questions?
- Do you think human beings are mainly self-interested or not?
- Do we have a 'natural affinity' for the suffering of others?

- Have you ever found yourself caught in binary thinking – where an event or person is either good or bad, right or wrong – with no room for 'grey'?
- Do you think life is merely about hard work?
- What might you do differently, if you had a chance to 'do over' your life?
- What brings out the best in you?
- Do you find it easy or hard to think of others, besides yourself?
- What do you treasure about your life?
- At the end of your life, how will you know you have been successful? Does wealth equal happiness?
- What are you looking for in your life?

CHAPTER 3

WORKING ON THE CHURCH'S MARGINS

Learn to do right; seek justice. Defend the oppressed. Take up the cause of the fatherless; plead the case of the widow. Isaiah 1:17

Having undertaken a brief review of historical philosophical thought over the centuries, I now look at the career of John Bottomley to understand how he came to incorporate so many complex and erudite notions into his reports. How did he move from ten years as a parish minister to a researcher, theologian, writer and critic of the times we live in?

I see John's career and work as having four phases, each building on the last with greater clarity of purpose. I describe them below, but to summarise: in the first phase he felt he had a calling and studied to be an ordained minister. He worked in a parish in suburban Melbourne. Outer suburban ministry meant John worked mainly with women at home with children and he barely saw the men of the local families as they spent their days in the workplace. He did this for nearly ten years and says himself that his training did not prepare him for the reality of the needs of his congregation. John says, *my professional role gave me tools to conduct funerals, but failed to equip me to understand my emotions* (Bottomley 2015:29). In *Hard Work Never Killed Anybody*, he writes candidly of delaying a visit to a parish family who had a dying family member. Admitting his fear of death to himself was the starting point of personal change. John acknowledges that he had believed fear to be a personal weakness and it was the enemy of his reason and therefore needed to be banished from his work as a minister.

People commonly feel that emotion must be banished, pushed aside, held at bay or ignored. But psychoanalytic theory suggests that this is not actually possible and neither is it healthy to try to achieve. There are many branches of psychoanalytic thought, but there is general agreement among them that investigating and seeking to understand emotional responses leads to growth and the only way to test this growth and learn these lessons is by experiencing them. Anything that is meaningful to us has emotional overtones: when we care about something, then emotional content is evident. But sadly, sometimes it is not clear to us that we are feeling an emotion, or what the feeling means.

Knowledge of this can only come with experience and reflection on experience. Often we can find ourselves feeling angry or upset with another person or a situation and we simply say that "he caused it" or "she is wrong"; rarely do we look inside to examine why the event caused such an outburst of emotion for us. Psychoanalyst Yiannis Gabriel writes...

Emotions suffuse all significant aspects of an individual's experience, including all meaningful objects, activities, and relations, and underlie virtually the entire edifice we call culture. Everything that is meaningful is also emotionally charged. Yet, emotions do not surface ready-made from the depths of the individual soul, even if this is exactly what an individual experiences when suddenly gripped by a powerful emotion, such as anger, self-pity, or despair. Instead, they are, to different degrees, learned, cultivated, modified, and suppressed throughout an individual's development. As such, they lie at the intersection of individual and culture (Gabriel 1998:312)

Phase One - The failure of leadership (1974-1984)

In the decade of his service as parish minister, John shifted from seeing himself as the parish leader to feeling a failure because he saw over time that he could not provide the leadership that seemed to be needed in his parish, to finally finding an accommodation of the emotion surrounding his departure from parish ministry. He writes in *Hard Work Never Killed Anybody* (2015:29) that he *saw in personal weakness a point of openness to Christ's love and forgiveness.*

It wasn't until he left his first parish that he saw the part he had played in accepting the traditional view of the religious ministry as a ministry to the local congregation and of himself as the 'leader' who could provide comfort and direction for any issue confronting his congregation. John wondered if he was the right person to lead the congregation, or if his own traditional view of the church and of family life was wrong. He ministered to wives at home, but the dynamics of their family life were unknown to him because the men of the parish were away for the bulk of the week at work and their private worries were largely not shared with him. He began to see that home life and working life were artificially kept separate and yet that they impacted on each other and that he was not in a position to solve private family issues. But he also saw significant failures in the parish system, reviewing his own understanding of his role and calling into question what could be achieved in a parish.

> Two fundamental views became crystallised for John at this time. First: home and work lives are artificially divided (as are home-based work and work outside the home) and that the supposed boundary is no boundary at all. Secondly: that people often seek a charismatic leader in whom to place their trust and they want to give over responsibility for resolving complex matters to that leader.

It is an untenable position to place all hope, faith and trust in one person to solve all dilemmas. Since no-one can live up to this fantasy ideal, they must inevitably fall short, make a poor choice or fail at some time. Frequently, instead of questioning the desire to have one person as an heroic leader, people tend to then blame the failed leader for the perceived failure. The leader is seen as at fault, rather than the concept of all encompassing, heroic authority. More will be said later in this book about the church and its capture to this dependent form of leadership.

The lessons John learned from full-time parish ministry are the pitfalls of accepting the view of your own power and leadership and the dangers of splitting issues of home life and working life. Home life and work life impact on one another; this seems unavoidable and yet it is largely denied in our modern society. Everyone brings their whole self to work, including personal worries, fears, plans and arguments from home. Yet it is typically thought of as wrong to do so. Why this should be, is of interest to me. The 'ideal' worker seems to be one who focuses on the work, commits to the mission of the workplace, aims to diligently progress the vision of the workplace and leaves all other goals and cares outside the workplace door. But clearly this is unrealistic. The boundary between home and work and the private and public domain is fluid and permeable.

In a report I prepared for CMN in 2015,[6] CEOs of large firms were asked about leadership at work. They were frank about how they felt they 'had to' behave at work. The separation of home and personal life from work is seen as the norm. But look at the words and phrases used by business leaders to describe their roles. They told me that if anyone wishes to be successful in business, they must play the game, work until they drop –

---

6   Not in print, but it formed the basis of the report called *CEO Insights* which can be found at http://www.afuturethatworks.org.au/reports

and if they drop then they are not resilient enough – leave their worries at the door, keep fighting, be tough as nails, keep going; pretend that they are in control at all times and these traits can mean they tend to be heartless. These are words actually used by the business leaders in answering questions about leadership. There is a clear sense that who they are at home is not be who they 'have to be' at work.

These respondents were CEOs of businesses and not-for-profit agencies. It is easy to think of the CEO as the person in charge, but these words and phrases from some of them would suggest they are not free agents. In the end, 88% of the CEOs commented that in reality, their relationships were the most important measure of their success with 28% of these specifically saying their family and 28% naming their children and wanting their children to feel proud of them. But what irony to want your children to be proud as you practise fighting, being tough as nails, heartless and pretending you are in control.

In that same report, CEOs were asked, "What keeps you up at night?". One CEO answered that people must earn things in life and it frustrates her that members of her staff do not take responsibility for their own issues and instead bring them to work. This frustration keeps the CEO awake at night. It is hard to know what is so emotionally disturbing for this CEO about her staff bringing their issues to work, and hard to see how they might be able to avoid doing so (by being an automaton?). Here is the individualistic viewpoint on show: people must earn things in life and, by implication, if they do not work hard to earn things, they must not complain. Again, we can see here that often we are not aware of the origin of what we feel or indeed that we are actually feeling something. While this CEO is frustrated at work that her staff members do not leave their worries at home, the knowledge of this comes into the private sphere of her own disturbed sleep at home. The anger of her reaction keeps her awake and so she responds but with little or no understanding of the connections her restless sleep is trying to get her to make.

In the 1970s, when John was a leader in his parish, there was limited scholarly debate about what it means to be a leader. Men were assumed to be natural leaders, while women stereotypically were nurturers and carers. A lot has changed in our views of leaders over the decades, but some gendered notions are resistant to change. The late 1970s and early 1980s saw an explosion in academic debate about what it means to be a leader. Debates first centred on the traits and later on behaviours that leaders exhibit, whether these be confidence, decisiveness, desire for power, intelligence, or initiative.

Later, the focus moved to the ability of the leader to influence and motivate others, with an acknowledgment of the impact of the situation surrounding the leader. The focus of leadership study became the capacity of the leader to be charismatic and to transform the lives and work of sub-ordinates. Further work on leadership emerged in the 1990s, highlighting the importance of social or emotional intelligence, which, it is said, is needed by a leader to engage and motivate followers.

Leadership debates still continue today with limited empirical evidence to support any single theory of what it means to be a good leader (see House & Aditya 1997 for a comprehensive review of the history of leadership studies). It is still typical to look to one heroic person, whether that person be the CEO or a minister of religion, to solve all problems, give us joy at work, offer experiences that challenge and engage. Really, this is fantasy. The Gallop[7] organisation has shown that only 13% of employees worldwide are 'engaged in their work'. (This result

7   https://news.gallup.com/poll/165269/worldwide-employees-engaged-work.aspx

is robust because it is based on a sample of 200,000 employees across 140 countries). Even more concerning is that 24% are actively disengaged at work. These employees are 'unhappy and unproductive at work and liable to spread negativity to co-workers'.

Robert Greenleaf postulated the notion of servant-leader in an essay he wrote in 1970. In that essay, Greenleaf (1970) said

The servant-leader is servant first... It begins with the natural feeling that one wants to serve, to serve first. Then conscious choice brings one to aspire to lead. That person is sharply different from one who is leader first, perhaps because of the need to assuage an unusual power drive or to acquire material possessions...The leader-first and the servant-first are two extreme types. Between them there are shadings and blends that are part of the infinite variety of human nature.[8]

This view of leadership is still current today and perhaps sums up changes in the way John has pursued his own leadership over his career, from having a sense that as an ordained minister, he is the congregational leader (the authority structure and ideology of parishes creates a leadership position for the minister and people expect to see leadership), to later working alongside those in need of support and encouraging their voices to be heard. He felt clearly that as minister, he did not have all the answers and came to see the accompanying feeling of powerlessness this realisation gave rise to, as a blessing, not a failing.

The stresses of being a leader can make people in those positions vulnerable to psychological defensiveness (Stein & Allcorn 2014), but this is rarely discussed in business literature.

---

8   https://www.greenleaf.org/what-is-servant-leadership/

The leader is typically exhorted to be tough, decisive, strong, logical, forward thinking, confident, visionary, authentic, committed, but at the same time a good listener, have empathy, social skills, be a motivator and focus on the transformation of others for the benefit of the organisation. If we think about it, how can anyone be all these things, to all people, at all times? It is a rather silly notion to expect and yet, this is how much of the language and literature on leadership is phrased. Luckily for John, his failure to live up to the ideal did not make him feel inadequate for long, but rather it led to a period of introspection. This led him to question the model, rather than his performance of it.

His public questioning of the model of parish ministry life began in 1982 in John's last year at Scoresby, with the formation of a men's group in the Scoresby congregation for the five weeks of Lent. If Lent is a season where the church seeks to turn away from sin, this was a Lent like no other in the history of the local church, where a group of men met to share their experience of pain and confusion over traditional masculinity with which they had grown up. Their shared experience of men's work and family in the light of their faith created a new sense of solidarity for John with other men. While the culture of masculinity/patriarchy has little or nothing to say about the men's confusion and pain, there was meaning to be found in their faith's permission-giving to share their stories without judgment. Through this small group, John learned something important about being accepted by God's grace as fully human, even when powerless. He recovered the truth that being powerless is part of the human condition, and how God's grace was revealed in the Lenten study of Jesus' passion, and death.

Three of the group went on to form the nucleus of a new group in Lent of 1984, meeting at the funeral parlour of one of the ministers in secular employment. It became the newly formed Urban Ministry Network. This encounter with the reality of death was also formative for John's later ministry with those bereaved by a work-related death. John remained a member of this group, meeting every fortnight for the next fifteen years. The other two founding members from Scoresby continue to meet with the group today. There is so little space or time for leaders, and for men more generally, to reflect on the stunting of growth that the roles our culture demand of us, whether as leaders or as fully human beings.

Interestingly, in Greenleaf's original essay he quotes Albert Camus the French philosopher (1913-1960) who said in his last essay called *Create Dangerously*

> *One may long, as I do, for a gentler flame, a respite, a pause for musing. But perhaps there is no other peace for the artist than what he finds in the heat of combat. 'Every wall is a door,' Emerson correctly said. Let us not look for the door, and the way out, anywhere but in the wall against which we are living. Instead, let us seek the respite where it is—in the very thick of battle. (Greenleaf 1970:38)*

In other words, Camus is exhorting us, paradoxically, to pause and think and stay inside those uncomfortable and difficult places, and not seek to avoid and leave them. John writes that by the grace of God he came to see that his fears were formed by being raised in a traditional masculine culture to be always rational, autonomous, secular and strong (Bottomley 2015:29). Greenleaf sees this view of pausing in battle as prophetic. It strikes me that this is the leadership that John Bottomley has tried to embody in his career: to speak from the complex, marginalised and difficult places of human life.

And it is what the psychoanalysts tells us: we must stay in those places of discomfort, listen to the voices within that tell us something is not right, investigate our emotional attachment to a position or idea and then act on what we see is not right. This is the prophetic vision in its truest sense. It is not about going out and converting people, but rather about investigating our own personal sorrow and then seeing its connection in others and in injustice in the world. In this way, the private and the public spheres are not separate, but united.

The Christian narrative holds these two spheres in solidarity, a unity forged by the prophetic vision of God's desire for justice and mercy. In this vision, grief is far more than an emotional expression. Here, grief is also a public lament that names what is unjust in the structures and beliefs of the modern world. (Bottomley 2015:30)

Phase Two - The value of work (1984-1994)

In the second phase of his work, John moved from parish ministry to take up ministry positions, first, with a church-based social research organisation, then as a researcher for the Urban Ministry Network Inc. with the Unions at the Naval Dockyards in Williamstown (in Melbourne). The workers were not aware that John was a minister and spoke with him about issues of justice at work. John listened to the issues raised by the workingmen and found a sense of calling there as he was accepted and embraced. This work became his life's work: ministry to the world of work.

John recalls a pivotal moment at the dockyards when a worker shared his lunch with him. Whilst John was an outside researcher and not privy to the dirty and dangerous work undertaken by the men at the dockyard, he was accepted and welcomed. He wrote a report on workplace health and safety issues at the dockyards. But more than this, he opened his eyes to the fact that work can injure and kill people. John's work at the dockyards gave him his first experience of solidarity with people who grieve over unjust work-related death and injury. He observed that their grief was private and not shared publicly. He saw that authorities were interested in facts and figures, but not the pain of personal stories of loss. Authorities wanted reports that highlighted improvements that could be made at the workplace to ensure better safety, but did not want to hear about the lasting sense of frustration and injustice that accompanied death at work from accidents that should never have happened or from industrial diseases such as the slow and tortuous death from mesothelioma.

This secular work at the Naval Dockyards in 1984 was the first project taken on by the newly formed Urban Ministry Network. The Network began as a group of Uniting Church ministers working in secular employment. Isolated from the institutional church, the group realised they were *being* the church in their daily work. As a part of its work, and to fund the organisation, the Urban Ministry Network developed and offered a specialised social research and development consultancy program on workplace issues.

In this second phase of John's working life, the focus on justice at work led to more reports and also actions that tried to bring the private suffering of unjust death into the public sphere through the setting up of an injured workers support group and an annual memorial service for families and workmates of those who died at work. The aim was to break the nexus of the private and the public and to lament these losses in the public realm and thereby to influence those in power to see the wrong being done.

During the late 1980s and early 1990s, John and colleagues undertook many research reports and activities to bring awareness of workplace suffering to the fore and to tell the stories of those involved. In 1988, John organised a Churches and Unions Working for Social Justice seminar and he wrote *We're all in the same boat*: a literature review on the role of support groups for injured workers as a preventative measure in community mental health. This report was funded by NHMRC Public Health Research and Development Committee[9]. In 1990, he co-authored *The Social Impact of Salinity on Farming Families in the Waranga and Deakin Shires*. This was a report for the Goulburn Social Development Council. It too brought together the workplace issues faced by farmers due to salinity of the land, detailing the personal and family suffering caused by environmental degradation.

However, economic conditions were deteriorating in the late 1980s and work for the Network was drying up. Support from the Uniting Church in Australia (UCA) remained out of sight. Serendipitously, John received an invitation from an innovative presbytery minister to consider a ministry position with an inner-city parish. In the negotiation that followed, John expressed his reservations about the traditional model of parish ministry, and the presbytery officials explained that they specifically approached John in the hope he could break open that model; otherwise, they stated they would recommend the parish's closure. John accepted a half-time ministry with the East St Kilda Parish (later St George's East St Kilda) on the proviso that the parish could allocate the other half of the ministry stipend to a 'creative ministry'.

In 1991, he wrote *Footsteps Back to Living: creating your own rituals and ceremonies for death and bereavement*. It was based

---

9   https://www.nhmrc.gov.au/about-us/leadership-and-governance/
     committees/research-committee

on interviews with over thirty bereaved people and provides practical advice for creating contemporary rituals for the grief journey.

Also in 1991, St George's Church established the Centre for Creative Ministries (CCM) as a ministry to and with the arts. The Centre developed a core of artists and interested people who began a dialogue around the arts and Christian faith. Catherine van Wilgenburg was appointed the first Coordinator of the Centre for Creative Ministries, Harris Smart was its second Co-ordinator and John became its third Co-ordinator when the Church Council decided to explore an amalgamation between the Centre for Creative Ministries and the Urban Ministry Network.

John's sermons were often grounded in his experiences of "working life" at the CMN or its predecessor agencies, or based on the narratives of people he met who shared their stories with him, particularly of deficiencies in "the system" which they were required to navigate following crises and trauma at work or at home. In this way, he was able to link Bible readings to concrete events and challenges in people's everyday lives in the here and now, and tried to bring a message of being understood, of comfort, of lament, and of hope in despair. John truly believes that God is always with us, and that God never deserts people even when they are suffering; this is what he tried to convey in his preaching.

In 2000, John began *Network News* (with the Network Chairperson, Barry Mitchell). It was a newsletter for the friends, clients and supporters of the work. Following UMN's amalgamation with CCM in 2004, *Network News* was replaced by *The Voice,* which also contained edited sermons, poetry, photos and film reviews. *The Work-Related Grief Support Newsletter* soon followed, with stories told by work-related grief clients. It was greatly valued by clients that they could see their stories in print.

John Bottomley, preaching
Image by Kate Dempsey

Other reports and activities in this decade include an annual Workers' Memorial Service at Melbourne's Wesley Uniting Church commencing in 1990, May Day services at the Victorian Trades Hall Council, and an Arts and Christianity Conference at CCM in 1993. While UMN developed its ministry with work and faith, CCM developed a series of ground-breaking initiatives for the arts and faith.

One example of how John connects the personal and political may be seen in his decision to introduce an annual service of thanks for nurses for International Nurses Day. He did this following his own life-saving surgery in 1993 to repair a damaged aortic valve and artery. The service began with a play commissioned by the CCM on the founder of modern nursing, Florence Nightingale. The Nurses' Choir provided music each year to enhance the array of speakers, touching for example on the spirituality of nursing, while lighting of candles of thanksgiving and prayers for nurses in their manifold circumstances were greatly appreciated.

John's surgery at that time was hugely formative as he came to see his heart as an interior life spirit. During his convalescence, he had a lot of time to think and reflect, and was surprised and quite shocked to discover that traditional rehabilitation services neither encouraged nor facilitated discussion of the big 'meaning of life' questions that his surgery had raised for him (and presumably others too), focusing rather on 'getting back to a normal routine and staying healthy'. The surgery and the wonderful care he received from staff at the Alfred Hospital, plus the experience of being completely helpless and dependent on others, re-formed John's previous thinking and he moved further away from traditional views of masculinity.

Phase Three - Creative Responses to Injustice (1994-2004)

During this period, John was preparing many reports related to workplace issues, but he was also exploring more creative ways of reporting the message of workplace injustice and finding ways to support victims of injustice, through his involvement with the Centre for Creative Ministries, an organisation established under the auspices of St George's East St Kilda Uniting Church where John was part-time minister for thirteen years. I call this period (1994-2004) the third phase of John's career. It was when creative projects flourished in both agencies. These included a Professional and Faith Development Round Table for CEOs in church community service agencies with Lonergan Enterprises in 1998; curation of the exhibition *Faith Works!* at the National Gallery of Victoria in 1998; two programs for men in management at a university on *Men's Health and well-being* in response to the suicide of a manager at the university in 1999.

It was also the time of the *Urban Dreaming Project*, comprising an art and music program with Aboriginal men and women resident in local St Kilda alcohol and drug recovery houses; an art program and a successful tour of six Aboriginal drug and alcohol recovery centres in rural and regional Victoria in 2003 and an art therapy workshop series for nurses at Epworth Hospital and another series for bereaved family members from the work-related grief support program.

In 1996, John facilitated the first support group for families bereaved by an industrial death with Industrial Deaths Support and Advocacy coordinator, Elizabeth Mobayad. In 1998, the Network employed Liz to research and write *'Til Death us do Part: industrial death narratives*, which covered ten healing narratives from families bereaved by a traumatic work death.

Through visual art, poetry and drama, John's work sought to listen to God's Word (presence) in the brokenness and grief of Indigenous people and those bereaved by work-related death. The art process aimed to facilitate the movement of God's Spirit towards healing, justice and reconciliation. The spiritual connectedness of Word and deed in the projects at this time was new ground for the Uniting Church in connecting the national problem of reconciliation with the trauma and grief of work-related death.

In uncovering how these two apparently separate experiences of suffering share a common rootedness in our society's two centuries of misplaced faith in the myth of economic progress, the work provided a practical model by which the Uniting Church can renew its commitment to be a truly national Church. Sadly, the Uniting Church is still yet to connect and take up the matter of colonial invasion and its impact on work-related grief and trauma. But I discuss this connection further in chapter four, *Major themes.*

In 2000, UMN produced a series of case studies of the impact of a workplace death on six companies in Victoria, called *I Think of Him every Day: Transforming the Grief Of Work-Related Death into Renewed Workplace Safety.* In 2003, CCM produced, *Winja Stories: Stories, songs and artwork from the Urban Dreaming Project participants.* The book was distributed to Aboriginal communities during the Urban Dreaming Project tour to regional Victorian centres.

This was a very productive period and included a significant report called *Work Factors in Suicide* (co-written with Margaret Neith and Elina Dalziel and published in 2002). This study was the first report to investigate findings of the Coroner's Court regarding death by suicide and to note the link between suicide and workplace stressors. Normally, a coronial inquest into a suicide death looks at general factors around the death, but does not put weight, specifically, on workplace worries nor ask if they might have been relevant to the death.

The report utilised secondary data analysis of Victorian Coronial findings on suicide cases between the years 1989 and 2000 where work factors were implicated. The data report is supplemented by case studies and an annotated bibliography. It found that over a decade (1989-2000), work factors contributed to the suicide deaths of 109 people in Victoria. Of the 109 cases of suicide investigated using the Coroner's records, 40% were known to have work stress or work problems (looming redundancy, long hours, changing work structures) as a contributing factor in their deaths. The report indicated that even this high figure is an under-estimation since the coroner's office did not keep a database to investigate these overlapping stressors on a person taking his/her own life.

> *"The report of the Urban Ministry Network on 'Work Factors in Suicide' is an innovative study of the part that workplace factors potentially play in suicide"*
> Graeme Johnstone, State Coroner (Bottomley et al 2002)

Work Factors in Suicide led to more formal studies being undertaken and that pioneering work is noted a decade later in both Routley & Ozanne-Smith (2010) and Routley, Trytell & Ozanne-Smith (2011) and led (in part) to a statement made in 2014 by Suicide Prevention Australia, specifically covering suicide and the impact of the workplace.[10]

In 2004 *Treated Like a Leper* was published. It was a survey of companies prosecuted after a work-related death, with

---

10 https://www.suicidepreventionaust.org/

a foreword by the Victorian Director of Australian Industry Group and the CEO of VECCI (Victorian Chamber of Commerce and Industry).

During this third phase of work, John became more engaged in developing workshops and liturgies to help heal the pain of victims. He offered a workshop called *Leadership as Calling and Task* for management at the Alfred Hospital in 2004 and a workshop called *Chaplaincy as Calling and Gift* for UCA chaplains in hospitals, schools and prisons in the same year. These were in addition to a *Recovery from a work-related death* workshop with Australian Industry Group and VECCI for their industry members. In 2005, John introduced Contemplative Worship two Sunday evenings per month. In 2006, five choirs, a kyoto player and an origami workshop leader contributed to the peace concert *Sing War No More* to mark the 60th anniversary of the atomic bomb dropped on Hiroshima. A donation was forwarded to the Japanese National Council of Churches for its ministry with children affected by radiation poisoning.

SING WAR NO MORE

A concert for world peace to commemorate

Hiroshima Day

Saturday 6 August 2005 8:00pm

at South Port Parks Uniting Church
319 Dorcas Street, South Melbourne

featuring
Koto Player, Miyama McQueen-Tokita
Origami Workshop, Fusae Nojima
and choirs
Loose Arrangement
Mood Swing
Resonance
Tongue and Groove
Yukari Echo

singing individually and together
of lament, solidarity and peace

And a message of peace from the Mayor of Hiroshima, Tadatoshi Akiba
read by Cr. Peter Logan

Proceeds support the National
Christian Council of Japan's support
and justice ministry for the hibakusha,
and the Creative Ministries Network
Peace Trust.

$10:00 adult
$5:00 concession
$25:00 family
Tickets at the door

This project has been
assisted by the City of Port
Phillip through its Cultural
Development Fund.

Inquiries: 9527 2283

Organised by the Creative Ministries Network, an agency of UnitingCare Victoria and Tasmania.

The flyer for a Hiroshima Day Concert for Peace.
Image by CMN

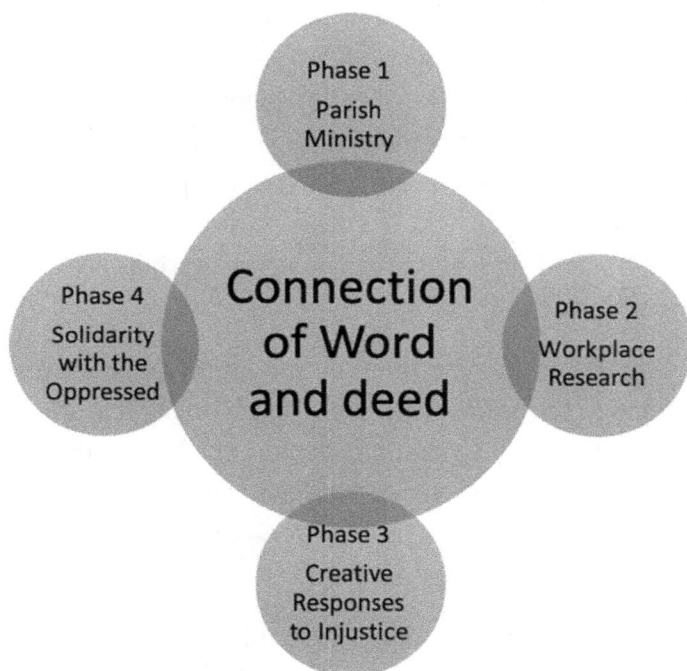

It was in this creative third phase of John's work that he commenced telephone support for the social justice work of Gippsland Asbestos Related Diseases Support (GARDS). This monthly support was funded by the Uniting Church. In 1996, the UMN commenced a work-related grief support program. At the end of 1998, a client of the support program, Bette Phillips-Campbell approached John to volunteer for the work-related grief support program and following eighteen months as a volunteer under John's supervision and training, Bette commenced paid employment half-time as the Coordinator of the Partnerships in Grieving Program (PIGP). From the beginning, the agency acknowledged that work-related deaths are traumatic for the relatives of the person who has died and for co-workers, but also for employers and managers. The grief support program exists today and (under different names) has been in existence for more than twenty years. It has evolved as a program of support and solidarity for families bereaved by a workplace death. The centrepiece of the program has been that the project worker is a companion in the journey of grief, not an 'expert' offering solutions.

The stated aim of the original Partnerships in Grieving Program[11] was to:

Establish a process of reconciliation between those families and workers bereaved by work-related deaths, and those employers and managers where a death has occurred who are responsible under occupational health and safety legislation for the provision of a healthy and safe workplace.

Over time, the grief support program moved to look more broadly at all instances of death at work and to include work-related suicide and exposure to industrial diseases. There is an important distinction between 'workplace death' (such as an accident that we may hear about on the news) and the more broad term 'work-related death', because workplace deaths only make up approximately 22 per cent (Naismith 2017:21) of all work-related deaths, and the government and media focus on these statistics to perpetuate a myth that harm at work is not widespread.

---

11 in 1999, the PIGP was evaluated by the Social Work Department of Latrobe University, as required by funding from the Department of Family & Community Services

Workplace Grief Support

The grief support program (with various names and funding sources over the years, especially from WorkSafe Victoria[12]) has taken the approach of the 'wounded healer' in the support it gives to clients (Nouwen 1979). It does not focus on apportioning blame for wrongful acts, it does not offer formal psychological counselling or medical intervention; rather, it offers a quiet form of companioning with the bereaved person, usually in their home, in whatever manner and time frame suits their needs. It aims to bring victims of workplace tragedies together in dialogue and understanding.

A fundamental part of the service from its inception has been public memorials and services of remembrance, which aim to make public the grief of families and to honour the death of loved ones in a way that calls for change to the way work is enacted. These activities encourage the participation of all parties in a process of healing, remembrance and reconciliation, including work colleagues and business owners.

The first remembrance service occurred in 1990, when the UMN initiated an ecumenical Memorial Service in Melbourne to remember workers who had died from occupational accidents and diseases. By 1997, the UMN had developed the grief support and advocacy program for families bereaved by work-related deaths. The connection of private grief with public recognition of death and commemoration and which includes both 'sides' to a work-related death is unique. The CMN workplace grief support program has sought to mend the split between the private and

---

12 The only annual funding was from the Victorian WorkCover Authority, also known at different times as WorkSafe Victoria. Grants from other sources were almost always for research, and some education, with small grants from the Share Appeal of the Uniting Church for art therapy programs and the memorial candle.

public spheres as these splits cause untold grief and lead to unjust events. The memorial quilt is another example of bringing the public and private worlds together in lasting memorial. Below is the prayer that dedicated the quilt at its unveiling.

PRAYER OF BLESSING AND DEDICATION

Let us pray, asking God to bless this quilt, as we dedicate it to the sacred task of a renewed commitment in our society to workplace health and safety.

Creator God, you pieced together the foundations of the earth, and stretched out the heavens. You hold all life from the beginning to the end of time in your love.

We ask your blessing on this Memorial Quilt.

We hold up before you those we love who have died from their work, and ask that they be at peace.

Bless all who have contributed their loving remembrance to this quilt, and wrap them around with your comfort and peace. By your tender mercy, thread their sorrow and grief into bonds of mutual support.

We dedicate this quilt to the task of strengthening our society's commitment to workplace health and safety. May the spirits of those we remember through this quilt inspire employers, unions and workers with an abiding reverence for the sacred dignity of human life in every workplace.

Amen.

The service model is not only unique, it is resistant to traditional methods of assessment, outputs and quantification: it does not offer a finite number of pre-determined sessions, covering specific topics. It does not follow the (now out-dated)

The Memorial Quilt, remembering people who have died at work.
Image by Gordon Traill.

model of grief[13] as something that is worked through and then let go of. Nevertheless, it is a vital and innovative model of support for the bereaved. It offers support to people as they undergo complex grief expression and as they deal with bureaucracies in determining compensation and cause of death. A recent survey by the University of Sydney[14] noted that less than 25% of respondents in their survey (which includes CMN clients) had anyone to help them navigate the complex workers compensation system.

The companioning support model is itself an alternative to the typical notions of theory of change, which can be reductionist and which lead to defining grief as something to be endured for a short period of time; which must be worked through in a linear fashion; which is private, not inter-generational and which is defined as pathology if not completed within a short time frame. The positive psychology approach, aims to minimise grief in 10-12 sessions with a psychologist or 16 sessions for so called 'complicated grief' (Wetherell 2012).

In a recent conference paper, I wrote[15] about the impact of neo-liberal thinking, that has entered the research on grief, the DSM (the Diagnostic and Statistical Manual of Mental Disorders), and funding processes for support services. For example, empirical research predominates in both death research academic journals, with quantitative methods outnumbering qualitative procedures 2 to 1(Wittkowski et al 2015).

I argue that the stages of grief are often somewhat trite in their depiction of the process of grief. The stages diminish

---

13 Hall, C (2011) *Beyond Kubler-Ross: Recent Developments in our understanding of grief and bereavement.* INPsych. https://Unitingcare.psychology.org.au/ publications/inpsych/2011/december/hall/ accessed Nov 2017
14 http://sydney.edu.au/health-sciences/research/workplace-death/death-at-work-report.pdf accessed Nov 2019
15 *The Business of Bereavement: Is grieving work that must be done?* Available from the author

personal agency, do not allow for public expression of anger, make grief seem linear and time bound. They speak of it as work that must be done by the bereaved, so that they may successfully get over the suffering and pain of loss of a loved one's death.

We "sequester" (isolate) death from life (Mellor & Schilling 1993) and this means we leave bereaved individuals to cope with their suffering in the private sphere. It is another form of the split previously referred to that so often occurs between the private world of emotion and the public world of rationality. We have funerals, yes, but even then, practices relating to death are controlled in a professional way, by doctors, coroners, undertakers and in the emotional response to death, by psychologists and counsellors. Grief is far more complex than a linear set of stages with specific emotional work tasks that are passively undertaken by the bereaved person, whereby they eventually become reintegrated into their usual working and broader social life - and everyone can put the pain of death behind them.

The recent bereavement exclusion in the DSM is a case in point: people experiencing grief can now be diagnosed as suffering a Major Depressive Disorder after two weeks of grief-related depression. On the other hand, families who accessed services such as the grief support program at CMN are *more satisfied with the support they received* through these services than the support they received through the formal system. They reported (Matthews et al 2012) that it offered support and understanding that they did not find elsewhere.

Newer theories of grieving indicate how socially constructed it is. Neimeyer and colleagues (2014:487) note that the expression of grief is 'dialectical, dialogical and dynamic'. Here is the Hegelian term dialectic used again. By this Neimeyer means that persons dealing with grief oscillate between wanting to be totally private or wanting to draw others into their grief; wanting

THE STRUGGLE FOR JUSTICE

to speak again and again of the loved one or not wanting to burden others with their grief; wanting to speak with as many as possible to try to find some meaning or understanding of what happened and why it happened and dealing with authorities who have their own ways of working and engaging with families. This oscillation is not time bound in a linear sense and this is respected and understood in the CMN grief support program. It is a way of looking at grief that is in keeping with the Hegelian dialectic described earlier, where meaning is constructed by people as they speak and listen and feel heard by others and as they go through the process of integrating the experience of death into their life narrative and as they try to construct meaning regarding the disruption that untimely death (in particular) causes. It is both private and public and the bereaved person is both the same and different following the tragedy.

The CMN grief support program does not exclude grieving families or individuals after a set timeframe. The Co-ordinator establishes a relationship of personal trust with the clients and often visits them in their homes. After two decades of service, she still has contact with 22% of clients (from time to time and at anniversaries of death). One of the key reasons that companioning support needs to take whatever time it does to support those bereaved by work-related death is that the legal and compensation system drags bereaved families through complex court matters that can take many years to play out.

One client of the program describes the unjust and drawn out process of court proceedings relating to a workplace death.[16] She says when the company responsible for her brother's death came to court ready to plead guilty, *they directed condolences to our family and appeared almost humble.* But it took twelve months for the case to come to court and the fine was a paltry $25,000.

---

16   See p. 102-107 of *Hard Work Never Killed Anybody*.

And then, subsequent to the court case, a new Director in the company was determined to appeal the severity of the sentence (although the company pleaded guilty). This meant the family was subjected to a further court case and dragged through their grief and trauma all over again. The client writes that the judge did not accept the appeal and the fine and conviction were upheld. *We emerged from the court victorious, yet feeling degraded and depleted of energy.*

With the assistance of CMN, this client was put in touch with the Managing Director of the business where her brother died. She asked to speak to him. He agreed to come to her mother's house to meet and talk. She says, *what a warm, caring compassionate person he turned out to be. He really restored our faith...he said I'm very sorry and he let us know Ross is not forgotten.* Later he sent the family a thank you note for meeting with him and a bunch of flowers. This man has visited many times since.

> Healing narratives provide bereaved people the opportunity to tell the story of their loved one's life and work-related death. Stories are documented either for personal or family use or for publication. An example of the latter is a book produced by the UMN and authored by Liz Mobayad, *Till death us do part: industrial death narratives* documenting the stories of ten families bereaved by industrial deaths.

When a loved one dies in traumatic, unexpected and perhaps unjust circumstances the level of grief can be overwhelming. This is largely because those who are left must somehow 'make sense' of the event, that does not appear to be fair or understandable. They must make sense again of life after an event that rips apart a view of the world as comprising a benign and random set of events: a family member goes to work each day and comes home each day. To hear that the loved one has died because of their work is incomprehensible, especially if the loved one is young. The trauma of a work-related suicide is also experienced as incomprehensible, and the widows in GARDS expressed similar trauma from asbestos-related deaths: working hard should not result in death.

The key thing to note in the story above is how *restored* the family felt by being able to speak directly to the employer and to hear 'sorry'. Grief Support Coordinator, Bette Phillips-Campbell, identified a number of cases involving clients such as described above, where people were waiting to see if the employer was to be prosecuted. The compensation system looks through the same binary lens that this book discusses. It is not meant as a criticism, as the coronial and workers compensation system do aim to improve systems and processes, but they do it by the means of finding fault and apportioning blame in order to offer redress. It is an indictment of a system built on the binaries of right/wrong and winner and losers.

The adversarial and drawn out legal compensation process made clients' grief more difficult, and it seemed that restorative justice practices might overcome some of these difficulties. CMN received a grant to research this idea and the report *Restorative Justice and Work-Related Death: Consultation Report* (Brookes 2009) was produced as a result. When bereaved families were asked, as part of the study, what they wanted following the death of their loved one, they identified six desired outcomes:

- Truth
- Accountability
- Acknowledgment
- Apology
- Reparation
- Prevention

They wanted a legal and compensation system that would achieve its own objectives: to establish the truth of the circumstances that caused their loved one's death; they expected that individuals would be held accountable; they wanted acknowledgment of the enormity of the harm done when a life is ended; to set appropriate reparation and to put in place effective prevention strategies. In other words, they wanted (a) an expeditious and fair legal process; (b) due recognition and involvement of the family; and (c) a legal outcome that would both convey the profound seriousness with which society regards work-related death, and to work towards ensuring something similar never happens again. The CMN report, authored by Derek Brookes, argues that most of these outcomes could be delivered by the legal system, although often they are not achieved because the system focuses on (another binary of our world) the adversarial system of justice.

Restorative Justice Project

The bereaved families in contact with CMN also had a larger view of justice than is currently offered by our justice system. They wanted outcomes that an alternative dispute resolution process, such as *restorative justice* is uniquely able to offer. This includes dialogue with family members after a work-place death by responsible individuals in the company. The families want to hear what really happened, rather than have the workplace reveal no more than would be in their legal interests to reveal and using lawyers to communicate the basics. They want representatives of the workplace to express, in person, a sincere apology to the family and they want to be able to express in person, the personal cost and impact of the company's actions.

They want, through this process, for the workplace representatives to come to a deeper understanding of the impact and to accept moral responsibility for their part in the death, rather than merely being found guilty (or admitting legal guilt) for having breached occupational health and safety regulations. Finally, they want the workplace to make amends in a way that would be meaningful to and beneficial for the family and other employees, rather than merely paying a fine to the government. These elements of justice help the family bereaved from a workplace death to have their dignity and respect restored.

CMN employed Derek Brookes (2008 and 2009) to review and recommend an alternative system of dispute resolution that could attend to the needs of all parties to the workplace death or injury. Brookes found that *almost everyone wanted a better way of dealing with the fatality. No one suggested that the current legal system should be entirely discarded or by-passed. But they did want it to be more effective, efficient and more considerate.* One concern that Brookes noted (from his interviews of clients, employers, family and colleagues) was the threat of prosecution if individuals offered a sincere apology (and fear that this could be taken as culpability). It was acknowledged that this possibility would mean both employers and work colleagues might be reluctant to meet with family members and speak openly about their part in what happened. It was suggested that a process of restorative justice should only occur after the coronial, WorkSafe or compensation legal processes had concluded.

The CMN work to progress a more inclusive and dialogic process of getting to the truth of a workplace death or injury began in 2008 and, in 2016, the Victorian Ombudsman (Glass 2016:14)independently took up the same challenge, noting that in 2014-15, her office received 503 complaints about the workers compensation scheme...*[t]he most common complaint (55 per cent) related to claims decisions and processes, including a failure to consider evidence in reaching claims decisions. The second most common complaint was about payments, including delayed payments and poor decision-making.*

Following this report by the Victorian Ombudsman, the Centre for Innovative Justice (CIJ) based at RMIT has been funded to: *Review the current dispute resolution model for workers compensation, in particular the process following unsuccessful conciliation, to ensure the model is fair and timely.*[17] The RMIT CIJ has contacted John Bottomley to speak about the CMN experience of restorative justice, as one of the few successful (and delineated) models of dealing with workplace death and injury that takes a holistic approach based on finding the truth, not on minimising and avoiding blame and culpability.

> The conceptual work of John Bottomley and his colleagues in the area of grief support, connecting suicide with work stress and the value of alternative dispute resolutions techniques such as restorative justice is way ahead of its time. Authorities are only now, some decades after the pioneering work, making the same links as can be found in this work.

The grief support program and its constituent elements of one-to-one companioning, clients supporting one another, newsletters published with stories of suffering and struggle, support for dealing with legal, coronial and compensation processes, ritual and public memorial and reparation is the culmination of the work of combining Word and deed for John Bottomley and best describes his commitment to healing the wounds of injustice; repairing the brokenness of splitting private

17 https://.rmit.edu.au/about/our-education/academic-schools/graduate-school-of-business-and-law/research/centre-for-innovative-justice/what-we-do/current-research/worksafe

and public spheres of life; finding creative solutions to complex problems; involving those damaged by the systems of our modern world by re-telling their narrative of loss and pain and finding unique ways to have their voices heard.

John's work shifted over time from giving a voice to those who suffer injustice at work in his research reports to offering creative outlets for the expression of their voicelessness, to walking alongside them in a companioning model of pastoral care. Along the way, he began to critique the role of the church in its complicity with upholding the idea that the social and economic system we have is the best and only system we can have. This critique will be discussed further in the following chapter, called *Major Themes*.

Phase Four – Solidarity with the oppressed (2004-2015)

In 2004, Creative Ministries Network became a UnitingCare agency with John as the founding Director. Since its establishment, it has had a focus on healing, justice and reconciliation. This is the beginning of the final phase of John's work. It commenced with creative work with war veterans and led to research and activities related to restorative justice and to the client-led grief support program described above. The wider CMN community and networks of academics, workers, agencies, both in the Uniting Church and from other denominations, were very important to John and an integral part of the CMN's life.

The *Basis of Union* that created the Uniting Church in 1977 calls the UCA to '*be in Christ a community of reconciliation, the beginning of a new humanity*'. The CMN argued that there is no greater need for reconciliation in Australia than between Indigenous and non-Indigenous people. After inheriting the former Centre for Creative Ministries' Aboriginal women's art program, CMN argued that the acute disadvantage experienced by Aboriginal people can be traced to their history of dispossession from their country.

The British colonial expansion into Australia that ruthlessly dispossessed Aboriginal people appears to be fuelled by the same faith in the myth of economic progress – the idea that the land must be productive. The needs of war veterans suffering post-traumatic stress disorder became apparent to the organisation at this time too. They, too, were excluded and carried a silent grief about their experiences of exclusion.

At the same time, more people die each year in Australia from work-related causes than the national road toll[18]. Most of these deaths cause suffering, felt injustice, and social division. CMN understood that, as an agency mandated to embody the beginning of a new humanity for those suffering dispossession, grief, injustice and chaos, it had a role to put forward innovative projects that tried to demonstrate the direct link between the pain and suffering of the dispossessed with the way post-modern capitalism understands the primacy of economic success. CMN aimed to develop innovative projects, which could become the model for how the Uniting Church in Australia could respond to the splits and binaries evident in our lives between the economic haves and the have-nots.

The spiritual connectedness of Word and deed in the CMN projects of the 2000s broke new ground for the Uniting Church in connecting the national problem of reconciliation with the trauma and grief of work-related death, that of war veterans. In uncovering how apparently separate experiences of suffering (work related death and the grief of war veterans) share a

---

18 https://www.actu.org.au/ohs/about-us/what-is-ohs This site estimates deaths from work related causes (illness and traumatic accident) to be of the order of 7,000 people annually in Australia, whereas the road toll was 1,135 in 2018 according to government website https://www.bitre.gov.au/statistics/safety/

common rootedness in our society's two centuries of misplaced faith in the myth of economic progress, the projects provided a practical model by which the Uniting Church could renew its commitment to be a truly national Church.

In 2003, the Uniting Church Share Appeal funded a project to provide creative writing and reflection workshops for Vietnam war veterans and their families. The project aimed to assist veterans to remember and reflect upon the impact of the Vietnam War on their lives. The project provided individual or small group tutoring in creative writing with published author and creative writing teacher Bronwyn Scanlon. Vietnam veteran Barry Pearce and his wife Sandra signed up for the project, and began meeting with their tutor, for nine two hour sessions.

Barry and Sandra's memories, ideas and feelings were explored through creative self-expression. The writing was reviewed and discussed each session with Bronwyn Scanlon, until a decision was made to produce the writing in book form. The resulting book, called *From Geelong To Nui Dat* was launched by Rt Revd Dr Peter Hollingworth in 2006.

In December 2004, CMN also established a monthly Contemplative Worship service with a small core group of veterans at All Saints Anglican Church in Newtown, Geelong. The Contemplative Worship service has been the heart of the creative activities that CMN developed to respond to veterans' concerns and which included a veterans song writing project and the creative writing project. The St George's Annual *Wounds of War* Service and the Remembrance Eve Dinner incorporating the Barry Pearce Peace Memorial Lecture also occurred in this phase of work.

The Uniting Church's Share Appeal funded a project in 2007, where a songwriter worked with veterans and their spouses, telling the stories of suffering from their war experience.

The narratives were then given to Fay White, a song-writer/ composer, so that she could transform them into songs for use by community choirs and congregations in worship. Fay conducted two workshops with members of *Veterans Faith and Wellbeing Support* and led a workshop at a retreat for veterans and partners to develop a collection of five songs. Fay's songs are titled 'Wounded', 'Eli Eli', 'Whatever we've done', 'Shona's song', 'Make your home in me' and 'The peaceable kingdom'. Through its projects with veterans and their spouses, the Creative Ministries Network identified that:

• addressing issues of guilt and forgiveness is important for veterans, irrespective of the date or duration of their war service

• when unable to work due to post-traumatic stress disorder, the question of vocation and God's calling emerges with fresh poignancy

• there is a challenge for veterans and their spouses to live in peace together while bearing the wounds of violence and war.

In 2007, funding was found for a Koori artist-in-residence in the Aboriginal Access Art Studio of Creative Ministries Network and in 2008, an art project explored three veterans' experience of war in Vietnam in the context of their lives. Lorraine Austin, Indigenous artist-in-residence at CMN, helped participants explore this theme through a series of conversations, drawings and art-making activities. Lorraine met with each veteran for two and a half hours, each month, over three months. She then worked in her own studio after each session, completing a large artwork relating to each story. A number of drawings and work-in-progress pieces were framed to set the context for the final exhibition of the artwork of the project. The exhibition of this work was held at the Uniting Church Centre for Theology and Ministry gallery. One of the three large art works was donated to the Creative Ministries Network for display in a public space.

Theatre Project - *Prophet and Loss*

In the latter part of the decade of the 2000s, the Creative Ministries Network began to seek funding for projects that aimed to test an integrated model of healing the suffering of injustice and offering hope of reconciliation. One such project sought to develop and perform a dramatic production interpreting the journey to healing, justice and reconciliation for businesses and families bereaved by a work-related death through the 'voice' of the Hebrew (Old Testament) prophet and poet Isaiah.

It is still significant today that the works that make up the Book of Isaiah reflected extensively on God's presence in the midst of devastation, grief and loss in Israel; and also proclaimed a vision of healing, justice and reconciliation for individuals, for Israel, for the nations, and the environment. The poetry of Isaiah identifies three themes that speak strongly to the contemporary experience of work-related death.

1. Israel is warned by the prophet that its misplaced faith in its neighbours idols of political power, technological sophistication and the pursuit of wealth will lead to suffering, injustice and death.
2. Israel is taken into exile – an experience of dislocation and grief, and the fear that Israel has been abandoned by God.
3. After a profound period of confusion, Israel is comforted by God and renewed as a people with a deep commitment to living in God's healing mercy

and justice. The task of living faithfully with God's promise is an ongoing challenge for Israel.

These three themes are also at the heart of CMN's ministry with families and companies bereaved by work-related death. The text of Isaiah illuminates the tragedy of work-related deaths as a religious issue, and invites a consideration of how God's desire for justice and mercy may address the culture, values, ethics and dignity of working life. Today, we believe in the idol of wealth with success measured primarily by material signs (a well-paying job, hard work, long hours, a big home, private schooling for the kids, an expensive car and so forth). We too suffer dislocation and grief, with anxiety and depression on the rise in the western world,[19] along with obesity and concomitant diseases such as heart disease and diabetes.[20] The work of the CMN reveals that we too are in a profound period of confusion and dislocation, just as Israel was when the Isaiah books were written.

The Isaiah theatre project began with the appointment of Jane Woollard as scriptwriter and director. In the first year, Jane researched Isaiah, interviewed CMN clients bereaved by a work-related death, and recruited the cast and production team. A showing of work-in-progress was held in June 2008 in Wyselaskie Hall, Centre for Theology and Ministry. CMN's commitment to involving the wider church in its projects led to an approach to the Centre for Theology and Ministry (CTM) to be a partner with the project, and an agreement that the end of the play's season would

---

19 https://theguardian.com/global/commentisfree/2016/may/07/mental-health-policy-anxiety-natasha-devon-young-people suggests that in 1980 4% of Americans suffered an anxiety disorder, but now nearly 50% do.

20 This article quotes the authority of the CDC in the USA https://medicalnewstoday.com/articles/278140.php and in Australia, the problem is highlighted in http://theaustralian.com.au/life/health-wellbeing/deadly-but-preventable-type-2-diabetes-on-the-rise-in-australia/news-story/932e3 6469eff636108e70be7617e026d

mark the beginning of the CTM's 'Wisdom's Feast'. This event took its theme from the play on work-related grief and Isaiah.

The play was called *Prophet and Loss* and it needed further funding of $39,000 to put the script on stage. CMN made submissions to twelve government and philanthropic funding bodies for this contribution, but none was successful. (CMN believed at the time that this failure to attract arts-based funding reflected a prejudice within the arts world against faith-based projects, as the scriptwriter had an impressive funding record with these bodies for other projects. Whether true or not, it does indicate the difficulty that funding bodies experience with projects that try to connect injustice with art and with faith).

> Evidence of binaries at work yet again is the fact that funding bodies and government departments find it so difficult to offer and support initiatives which bring parties together over divides, which fuse art and science, which speak to the public and the private spheres of life and which heal wounds caused by separation. Looking at life as a complex, mature evocation of spirit, whether rational or creative, seems so difficult.

Just when it seemed the actual production of the play would not go ahead, CMN received an anonymous donation of $30,000 from a church couple who had learned about the project. This was a gift of grace, and ensured the project could proceed. The donors made themselves known to CMN at one of the performances, and when they learned of a supplementary project to make a documentary film, provided a further donation of $10,000.

A still from the play, Prophet and Loss
Image by Ponch Hawkes

One key strength of the creative projects of CMN during this phase of John's work was the capacity to pay participating artists, art teachers, actors and scriptwriters a fee appropriate to their profession. The respect given to all the artists was a significant reason that the task of integrating their art within CMN's faith perspectives was possible and a key focus of John's aim to model and support just and fair employment. According these artists respect as professionals assisted CMN to sustain open and honest communication about issues of artistic development, interpretation, and encouraged them to contribute fully to the project's development.

But this sophisticated project had distinctly humble beginnings. A staff member asked at a staff meeting, 'what does it mean for us to be a prophetic ministry?' John considered this question and took it to a meeting with Howard Wallace, the Professor of Old Testament at the Uniting Church Theological College, and Howard suggested John begin by reading an article and a book on the prophetic literature in the Book of Isaiah. After John discussed his reading in relation to the issues facing Urban Ministry Network, Howard invited John to speak at his Isaiah class about how this ancient text informed contemporary questions of ministry.

Howard was particularly intrigued by John's concerns about the governance issues that were facing the Synod and the UMN agency at that time and how they resonated with Isaiah's various affirmations about God's governance in the troubled times facing God's people, Israel. This prompted Howard to ask John if they could work together on a peer-reviewed article for a journal. Howard suggested he apply for a small research grant to fund John's time on the project, and thus began a unique partnership in the Uniting Church between an academic and a practitioner with a common concern for discerning how contemporary prophetic ministry may be shaped by fidelity to the biblical text. Their article was published in the 2007 issue of *Uniting Church Studies* (Wallace & Bottomley 2008).

The integrative task of combining Word and deed deepened with Howard successfully applying to the Melbourne College of Divinity for small research grants over the three years of the Isaiah project to research emerging issues of interpretation on work in the prophetic perspective. John Bottomley was engaged as the research consultant for these two small grants, and wrote papers in collaboration with Howard on governance in community services, worship in UnitingCare agencies, vocational issues for UnitingCare CEOs, and the contribution of Isaiah's penitential prayer to understanding the causes and treatment of post-traumatic stress disorder. A proposal for gathering this material into a book was submitted to Uniting Academic Press. The resulting book is called *Hope for Justice and Reconciliation* and it included publishing the script of 'Prophet and Loss'. (See Wallace & Bottomley 2011).

The book written by Howard Wallace and John was the culmination of John's wish over many years to articulate the work of CMN and its predecessor agencies as a bringing together of faith and work, with God's governance at the centre.

One of the book's chapters focused on the governance framework that UnitingCare required of all its agencies from 2001. The chapter argues that the governance tools that were required to be implemented by organisations affiliated with UnitingCare arose from a view of humankind as rational, autonomous and in control of the environment. They are also imbued with a fear of risk. Corporate governance policies and procedures were seen to be needed to minimise the risk of failure or loss. More will be said about this approach to governing community service organisations in the next chapter. Suffice to say here that the chapter argues that the theological underpinning of the UnitingCare agencies was ignored in favour of implementing a typical business model of governance (the Carver Model) and that this was flawed. The chapter re-states the question that Isaiah posed of Israel: *what risk management strategy for God's people will manage the consequences of their shifting allegiance from God's governance of their life and purpose to a theory that claims for itself universal status?*

This question was not simply an academic question for the Board and staff at CMN. Staff meetings began with a time for staff to share a reflection on 'what has nurtured or troubled your spirit in the past month or so?' John was keen to encourage staff to begin meeting under a sign of God's goodness in creation rather than have them believe they had to live and work in a problem-focused environment. He helped staff in a very practical way to focus on God's abundant creation, not capitalism's notions of scarcity. This flowed over into his welcome to staff to share their personal spirituality, and to reflect on what their spiritual convictions might bring to their self-understanding and work practices. And staff were encouraged to see their work as a vocation or calling, so in the final years before John's retirement, staff agreed to implement a 'vocation review' with John rather than the traditional performance management regime.

But it was the Board of CMN that held the question of God's governance of the agency and the created order to its heart. Soon after a particularly painful time in the agency's history, the Board began the practice of having a time of theological reflection on their work at the end of their meetings. One series of meetings had Board members sharing their experience of the Spirit in their work. The 2013 Annual Report noted: *'this commitment is often a struggle for Board members, and (we) also affirmed the value of the struggle to bring our concerns before God through intentional reflection and/or prayer.*' The Board replaced their Strategic Plan with a Directions Vision framed by the journey of Ignatian spirituality. The cycle of reflection and action offered here in this book is based on the same Ignatian principles.

> The Board and staff at CMN enacted an integrated way of being 'church in the world'. They did not rely on business models of rational planning, but rather took a more reflective and contemplative route to their work with those who suffer and are marginalised.

Board members attended annual faith-reflection retreats on being a community of reconciliation in Christ, sculptured their faith journey after the pattern of Stations of the Cross, and further explored reconciliation through smashing tiles and creating a personal mosaic. All of their annual faith exploration was bookended by an annual founders' day anniversary celebration in February and the remembrance service for those who died from work-related causes each November from 1990 to 2014. From this fertile soil, perhaps it is not surprising that CMN would in 2011 give birth to the first UCA congregation that was part of the life of a Uniting Church agency.

While the agencies John worked in were considering reflective practices and inclusive ways to combine faith and action with a dedication to their calling as a prophetic ministry in the world, corporate re-structuring of government bureaucracies to be more efficient and emulate the private sector began in earnest in the 1990s in Australia and elsewhere around the world. In the 1990s, the State government authority, Melbourne Water, corporatised, following the model of the private sector and began a program of redundancies.

Melbourne Water lost some 6,000 employees over the decade, with a massive 31% decline in one year alone.[21] *During the time of these redundancies, three Melbourne Water staff took their own lives.* Something is profoundly wrong when a person's work contributes to their death (by accident, illness or suicide) and this tragic situation was taken up by John Bottomley in his report funded by the UCA's Hotham Parish Mission and published by the Union Research Centre on Organisation and Technology called *The Pressure is Enormous: the hidden costs of corporatisation* (Bottomley 1997).

In that report, John noted the conflict between the opportunities of a free market to make profit and the fundamental dignity of people at work. The work was prophetic as it so starkly delineated the role of public entities (water, transport, energy, gaols) as services for people, not for the profit of private companies at a very early time. The myriad costs of privatisation of essential services are still being felt in our society now.

CMN drew upon arts-based ministry projects with Indigenous people, veterans and those bereaved by work-related deaths to make connections and build links between theology and action in order to link different experiences of suffering, injustice and trauma to the function and meaning of work in our economic system. The projects not only held the deep pain of participants, but through the use of art, transformed often violent and traumatic stories into experiences of exquisite, profound and, at times, disturbing beauty. The funding received also supported reflection upon the projects, which has identified seeds of new models for the church to engage with the world of work.

---

21   Melbourne water Annual Report 1993-94, p. 2 as cited in Bottomley J.K (1997) *The Pressure is Enormous: the hidden costs of corporatisation* Union Research Centre on Organisation and Technology Melbourne, Australia.

"The lights dimmed. This was the moment we were waiting for. We did not know what was in store. On this wintry night, the Wyselaskie Hall transformed into a sacred place to express the intense grief, anger, sense of bewilderment and incredible resilience of those who have lost loved ones in workplace accidents.

"We were drawn immediately into these stories through actors who became one with the story, who put on the mantle of grief and pain, who with great integrity and sensitivity wore the garments of mourning and lived out the experience before our eyes. We saw the mood changes of the bereaved, the unique way each person dealt with the experience, and the efforts of those reaching out to them. We experienced the impact of the inflexibility and coldness of systems and processes unable to respond with any compassion."

Extract of a review of 'Prophet and Loss' written by Charles Gibson, Acting Director of UnitingCare Victoria and Tasmania and his wife, Margaret

The Creative Ministry Network listened over many years to people bereaved by work-related death and through that deep listening they discovered that most of those who die (despite popular misconceptions) are people who have worked hard. They had worked hard to build their identity as people of worth, to provide financial security for their families and for their futures. Many have put their faith in the myth of economic progress, trusting their hard work to bring them a reward.

CMN research has found similar beliefs amongst employers striving to build their business, leading to lack of safety awareness, or placing a higher priority on production than safety. Sadly, the misplaced trust of many in our society on the promised fruit of hard work has caused an accumulation of risk factors, with tragic consequences.

Injured workers and the compensation system

In 2014, CMN undertook a comprehensive review of the experience of long-term injured workers with the compensation system in Victoria, Australia. The report is called *Filling the Dark Spot* (Pollock et al, 2014) and it found that receiving compensation after workplace injury is certainly no simple, straightforward process. The report notes that whilst workers were able *to access assistance with the technical aspects of the workers compensation process e.g. through their union or legal representation, they seemed particularly ill-prepared for the emotional experience of the system* (p. 37).

Whilst the report noted some positives regarding injured workers' experience of the compensation system, workers overall experienced the system as unfair and unjust. They felt that it prioritised employers' interests and did nothing to improve the situation that had caused the injury in the first place.

> The majority of workers in the report said they had been treated disrespectfully, dismissively or without humanity by the workers' compensation system.

The interviewed workers also reported inefficiencies and errors in their cases and noted that the complex requirements of the system combined to create a sense of being trapped. They were not prepared for the evidentiary and adversarial nature of the process. Overall, workers struggled with the requirements of the process and found that speaking with a peer who has experience of the compensation system was most helpful to them, as provided by the CMN grief support program noted above.

At the core of the suffering, despair, and confusion heard in its client groups, CMN has seen the 'dark side' of the modern industrial world of work - with its reliance on Enlightenment beliefs in science, technology and progress to the exclusion of all else. CMN declared the tendency in our culture to reify these beliefs is a form of 'bad faith', and stated its view that priority should be given to proposals for action in the Church that boldly witness to radical faith in God's love for the world and show the way towards the unification of Word with deed in building a new future for humankind.

CMN activities, research and client work all had at their core a sense of being 'faithful to the God who has called' (see Synod's *A call to the Church*). CMN aimed to directly confront and address the deep-seated resistance in both church and nation to listening to the long-suffering grief of Indigenous and non-Indigenous people caused by our society's blind devotion to the myth of economic progress.

It is a matter of faith in Jesus Christ that the CMN sought God's justice in the world through listening to the brokenness of people whom our society has cast off. Creative Ministries Network discovered the value of the arts in creating a safe space for listening to painful narratives, then transforming the darkness of grief and despair into something powerful, beautiful and hopeful. CMN was founded on the value of listening for God's Word in the lives of the disenfranchised and saw this listening as a matter of faithfulness to the Holy Spirit. In its foundation, CMN held the view that it is within the painful narratives of death, dispossession and trauma that the seeds of God's new life in Christ are disclosed.

The consistent thread of the three agencies over time (Urban Ministry Network, Centre for Creative Ministries and the Creative Ministries Network) was to be active in the world, bringing about hope and heeding the call to fight injustice. But its actions did not arise from any secular notion of 'helping the poor' or any political ideal, but rather as a call from God that this is what is required. The agencies put into practice the unification of Word and deed; not word and deed, but Word and deed. The Word is the call from God that faithfulness to God's plan for humanity will bring about justice and mercy and that action is required in the world to bring it about. But we must listen to hear the call.

The work has emerged from thirty years of listening, solidarity, and shared activity with people who are all equal before God. It puts into practice the Aboriginal word *dadirri*, from the Daly River People of the Northern Territory. It was mentioned in the Introduction to this book and is described in more detail in the following chapter. It is inner deep listening and quiet, still awareness. Dadirri[22] recognises the deep spring that is inside us all. We call on it and it calls to us. It reminds us that all persons matter and all persons belong.

Indigenous researcher Judy Atkinson wrote a book about applying the idea of dadirri to our day-to-day work and to research with marginalised groups. She says that if we research with dadirri in our hearts, then we listen first, gain respect and trust before we can hope to offer help or solutions. In research, dadirri offers

- a knowledge and consideration of community, and the diversity and unique nature that each individual brings to community

22 http://nextwave.org.au/wp-content/uploads/Dadirri-Inner-Deep-Listening-M-R-Ungunmerr-Bauman-Refl.pdf

- ways of relating and acting within community
- a non-intrusive observation, or quietly aware watching
- a deep listening and hearing with more than the ears
- a reflective non-judgmental consideration of what is being seen and heard; and, having learnt from the listening, a purposeful plan to act, with actions informed by learning, wisdom, and the informed responsibility that comes with knowledge.[23]

But listening with dadirri in your heart is not a research 'technique', for at its depth, dadirri knows the value of mystery and the sacred quality of boundaries in personal and community life. This was brought home to John in a project with an indigenous colleague and researcher. John employed a young indigenous colleague, Garry Deverell, to research Aboriginal leadership in the Uniting Church. John has told me that the contract he put forward for the research put Garry's position as researcher at odds with being an indigenous man. The critical reality for John was to take responsibility for what had (unknowingly) occurred and for the pain caused by the conflict between being part of a community and an 'objective researcher' of it. From that point forward, the question of the research focused on why John had put the researcher in this position. As they discussed this together, and later at the Board, it was agreed that CMN staff and board had learned more than anyone else about the impact of colonialism from engaging with the project, and that is why the report was published as John's report, (Bottomley 2009) with Garry's advice and assistance.

---

23 https://lowitja.org.au/using-dadirri-research-methodology

The western mantra is that 'knowledge is power', but in the world of dadirri, knowledge is also the privilege of being fully human in powerlessness. It is the silence that respects and holds in confidence a shared trust that cannot be spoken or indeed, acted upon. John learned this in pastoral ministry on countless occasions: when the wellbeing of another depends on a shared story being held in confidence. But it came as a shock to learn this new dimension of the boundary between colonial and Aboriginal societies. The politics of western research does not have privileged access to indigenous worlds as of right, and it was the grace embedded in dadirri that allowed John to embrace that humbling truth about the limits of his experience and understanding.

I think it is correct to say that, especially towards the end of his working career, John Bottomley undertook his research with a sense of dadirri in his heart in much the way that Judy Atkinson has outlined. It is something to strive for in Uniting's work, that agencies work alongside those they help, by first listening to their stories, being open to seeing and feeling the connection we all have with one another and moving into a non-judgmental space of true hearing. From this space, action that is congruent with need can arise.

Reflections on the material in this chapter

This chapter summarises the career of John Bottomley and the Urban Ministry Network, Centre for Creative Ministries and finally the Creative Ministries Network, dividing the work into four phases. First, it recounts nearly a decade of parish ministry, secondly a decade of workplace research, thirdly a rich phase of research, writing, art, music and performance and finally a fourth phase of peer support, companioning of victims of injustice and a call for the powers that be, including the Church to stand with the oppressed and change the way we live.

- Can you see phases in your own work history? What marks them?
- Have you come closer to your goals in your working life, or are you 'just treading water'?
- Have you ever felt a call to do something more?
- What might you do to change things?
- Has your work allowed the voices of the voiceless to be heard?
- Have you been creative in your approach to your work?
- Have you found ways to connect public expressions of solidarity with private suffering that you have encountered?
- Have there been times when you struggled to stay engaged and focused?
- What has been the highpoint of your career to date?
- Have you used dadirri (or something like it) to calm and still your responses to the busy working day?

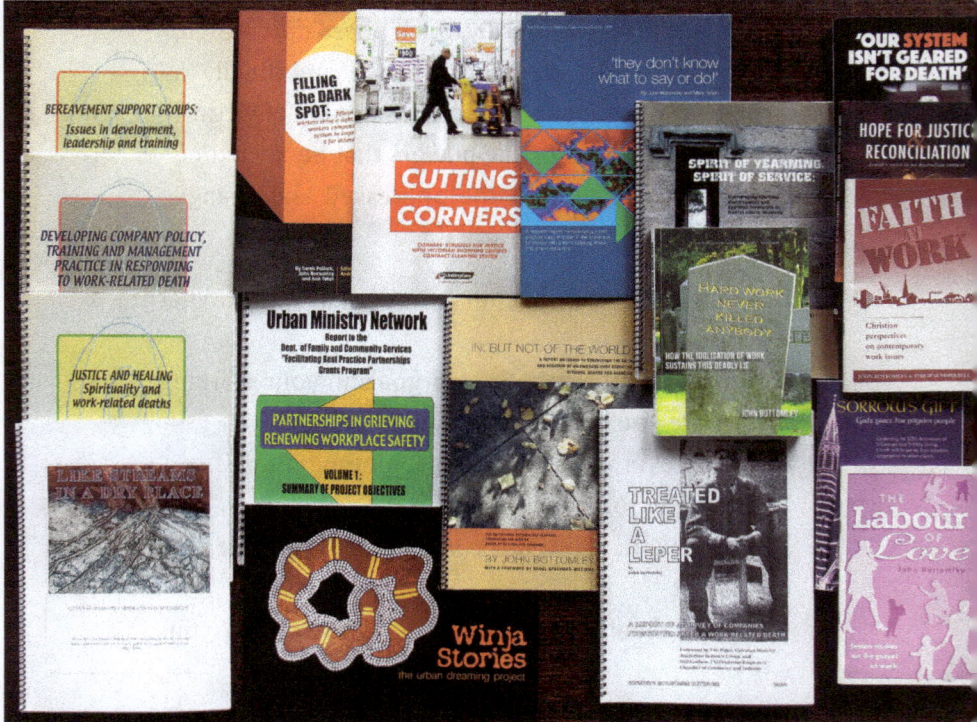

A sample of some of the reports and books written by John Bottomley and colleagues. Image by Andrea Colvin Photography

CHAPTER 4

MAJOR THEMES

God is still calling the church today to this prophetic ministry, calling agency boards, staff and congregations to learn a model of pastoral care that may comfort and witness to a people captive to their religious devotion to idolatrous beliefs about work. (Bottomley 2015:18)

In the previous chapter, I outlined the work John (and colleagues) undertook and the path taken over many years of research to highlight injustice and stand in solidarity with those seeking justice. In this chapter, I try to group the main themes of that work as I see them and offer a summary of the ideas tackled in over eighty different reports and three books. My aim is to make the ideas accessible to a new audience and to bring to the attention of Uniting (and others interested in the big issues surrounding the meaning of our lives), the dire need of looking closely at the way we live now and making linkages with the impact of the way we live on the earth and its continued sustainability. It will become clear that the brief outline of the history of philosophical, psychological and political thought in Chapter two, *A Consistent Thread,* will stand us in good stead for this discussion.

While John's work ranges across many topics, his themes are mainly centred on the dignity and respect of the person and this is discussed primarily in relation to the world of work. But John's work draws links with history, politics and theology in making the case that the way we live today damages people and relationships.

His writing suggests that at the heart of issues in Australia (and other colonised nations) is the denial that white Europeans invaded this land and seized control of it from its original inhabitants. Succeeding generations have profited from this theft, but this is largely denied. It is the first lie we tell ourselves in regard to our autonomous, independent hard working selves. Australia has never been a 'level playing field' of endeavour where hard work is rewarded and everyone has equal access to the wealth of the nation. From invasion, it has been a land of privilege for the few; and poverty and disenfranchisement for the many. Shortly I will speak more of this unspoken history and its impact on us now. But, first, I will outline in brief the other key issues John raises and then comment on each in turn.

1. Australian history and industry founded on a lie

2. The disease of modernity – profit over people

3. The dignity of the person lost

4. Binaries – abundance vs. scarcity, private vs. public

5. The orthodoxy of self-interest

6. Inability to think (reification, ideology and hegemony)

7. The failure of the church to call for change

The second key theme of his work is what John calls the 'disease of modernity' - the focus on private wealth and profit often at the expense of people, connection and relationship. This focus on the material world, on profit, on economics leads us often to see others – and indeed ourselves – as commodities to be bought and sold. Karl Marx called this commodity fetishism. A fetish is an object that we imbue with value and power beyond its original purpose or meaning. In capitalism, we make commodities (anything that can be bought or sold) things of high value, give them deep importance and fill them with meaning. John would say this is idolatry: putting things above God.

In an article on Marx's concept of commodity fetishism, Burris (1988) argues that in capitalism, people are alienated from their true selves as they come to be seen (and to see themselves) as merely the sum of the things they own, buy or sell. And, further, that the relationships between people in a capitalist system, are subordinate to the buying, selling and valuing of things (not people). People are not as important as things.

Persons are thus reduced to functioning as representatives or "personifications" of the things in their possession, while productive relations among them become dependent upon the market relations that are established among those things (Burris 1988:6)

Sadly, when people are thought of as commodities, they are more likely to be treated as objects. In the treatment of others are objects, we can use them, abuse them, exploit them or dismiss them. Here is where John speaks of the loss of dignity and respect for people as God's creation. He argues that the putting of profit before relationships with people leads inevitably to the loss of dignity for people. Following this idea is the second lie we tell ourselves, that those who have 'fallen through the cracks' of our system have been either unlucky or, more likely, indolent and brought their circumstances upon themselves.

This narrative helps to keep the truth at bay which is that at any time something could happen to any one of us to cause us too to be in grief, suffering loss or injury. It leads us to binary thinking. Binary thinking is seen in the uncomplicated opinions we hear these days, in phrases such as calling refugees economic migrants, or illegals, boat people, or queue jumpers or those without a job dole bludgers, or leaners. It is a false dichotomy, but it provides an artificial distance between 'us and them'. Binaries keep issues simple and they make it easy to demonise others. As noted in chapter two, western systems of thought from the Greek philosophers and in the Enlightenment period tend to train us to think in binary opposites: if one side is right, then the other side of the argument must be rejected as incorrect.

The fifth big issue that John investigates is the orthodoxy of self-interest in capitalism. In capitalism, it is assumed to be true that everyone acts with self-interest. As discussed in chapter two, the essential nature of humans as either inherently self-interested or essentially concerned for others has, in fact, never been clearly defined by historians or philosophers. This is, of course, because we are both - depending on the situation we can act in either or both ways. It is another example of binary thinking to consider humanity as only self-interested (or indeed the counter view that we are only concerned for others). Self-interest is considered in economics to be the motivator for buying and selling. And furthermore it is assumed that people act rationally in their own self-interest. These are basic tenets of capitalism, which will be discussed a little more below.

John argues that the system of capitalism that we all work under is so pervasive, so all-encompassing in its reach that we are unable to see its hold over us. We cannot imagine any other economic system, we cannot believe that strangers would care for us and not expect payment, we use business and economic language in our everyday lives and in church documents without seeing that it does not necessarily belong. The hold on us is so strong that we even struggle to comprehend that we are destroying the earth and overusing its finite resources and that, if something is not done immediately about this, we will all perish. It is astonishing, really, that we fail to grasp the implications of not doing enough to end poverty, re-distribute wealth and save the planet.

Reification is a term not often used these days but it means making an abstract concept — falsely and mistakenly — into a concrete thing. So for example, a concept such as love may be reified these days by the showy display of an expensive wedding. The concept that is signified becomes only the material or concrete thing that we see and the true meaning of the concept is thereby lost. Similarly, money becomes a symbol for happiness, when clearly it does not necessarily bring happiness and as a concept happiness is much broader than that. In modern times, we reify work, we are captured by the language of business and the discourse is hegemonic – it renders us unable to think of a different way of being human.

Finally, John calls on the church to open our eyes to the hegemony of capitalism and show us that we can hope for and build a better world. He argues that this has been the role of the church in previous times, but not anymore. The church is captured by the prevailing ideology of modernity and it too falls victim to business discourse and the splitting of public from private, acting in a self-interested way to sustain its own institutional structure and place in society and thereby no longer fulfilling its prophetic role.

Now I turn to explaining each of the seven themes in more detail, starting with the founding of modern Australia on a lie.

1. Australian history and industry founded on a lie

Australia's history is alive and well in the cultural psyche: John argues that acquiring land in Australia from its indigenous inhabitants, with no acknowledgment, has left scars that can't heal, while we continue to deny the truth of that history. The legal invention of *terra nullius* was in place until 1992. In the past 200 years, Australia has grown and prospered, but at a cost.

This land was not empty and farms and industry were developed on stolen land. We all know this dark truth. We fundamentally deny the injustice on which this nation's prosperity is founded. Whether any of us individually and living today has hurt an Aboriginal person is not the point. The point is that we immigrants to this country have all prospered from the fiction that the country was empty and unoccupied when British settlement began. The nation has been built on a lie and we continue to live in a divided country because of it.

We know the country is not as it once was before European settlement, we know that all white settlers and immigrants have been here for a just a very short time in comparison to the first inhabitants. Whether we believe the atrocities of the past have been exaggerated or not, we all know that Australia is not as it was in the millennia before white settlement.

These truths call the sovereignty and legitimacy of white settlement into doubt. Our sense of national pride is compromised by this truth. We try to separate 'Aboriginal problems' from the rest of our society, but we perceive, perhaps dimly, that they are linked. It is yet another example of how we try to create artificial dualities so that they are more easily separated from each of us, pushed away from view and for which we each do not have to take responsibility.

But in the first chapter of their book, Howard Wallace and John Bottomley (2012) quote Jesuit John Wilken to sum up their argument for non-Indigenous Australians that responsibility for the totality of our nation's past is ours to accept:

> ... *thus we Australians today cannot say that what was done in the past is no concern of ours. As people living in history, we bear the burden of the crimes of the past – just as we are enriched by the grace which was present also in the lives of our predecessors. True reconciliation can come about only if we humbly and honestly accept that burden.* (Wilken 1992:69)

In a recent essay, Tony Hughes-D'Aeth[24] calls agriculture in Australia a religion. He notes that white Australians tend to look back at Australian history (through rose coloured glasses) as we reflect on the farmer, the stoic man of the land: taming the land, battling drought, overcoming resistance and building the country from agriculture, livestock and extraction of resources. But, of course this too is a lie, not just given the fact that some early settlers (and later returned soldiers) were given land, while others simply took it (the squatters), but embedded in the lie is the notion that it was only when Europeans arrived that the land yielded up its resources and became productive and useful.

There are many books and reports now indicating that the ancient Australian land has for the most part been ruined by post-industrial farming, whereas in contrast the land was used and sustained for at least 60,000 years by its first inhabitants. Europeans brought their ideas to a foreign place with the supreme self-belief that what they knew was right for this place

---

24 https://theconversation.com/friday-essay-dark-emu-and-the-blindness-of-australian-agriculture-97444

too. We now suffer extinction of local species from introduced species, hooved animals compact our soft earth and cause water run-off and silting of rivers, which, if they are not re-directed for irrigation of crops that do not belong here, are full of carp, with native species finding it hard to survive. Just as *terra nullius* was the lie that the land belonged to no-one, so the notion that Australia's First People's did not work the land is also a lie.[25]

Traditional indigenous peoples embraced all life as part of a complex system of relationships which can be traced directly back to the ancestral Spirit Beings of The Dreaming. This structure of relations had the result of maintaining ecological balance and an economy of abundance in the indigenous world. But colonial society was blind to Aboriginal culture by the colonialists' belief in the virtues of hard work, the power of rational thought, the advances of science and opportunities provided by technological innovation (Bottomley 2015:113)

If our economy is built on a lie, then everything we achieve and gain is tarnished by that lie. Burying the reality of Aboriginal people's experience of death, illness and grief in the name of economic progress has also contributed to the denial of these same truths in the working lives of all Australians. For example, for many years the Australian Heart Foundation opposed any acknowledgement of the link between work stress and the high incidence of heart disease amongst Australians. But we know now that stress has a very clear link with heart disease and John traces a connection with the same refusal to acknowledge the prevalence of heart disease in the indigenous community as resulting in part to the stress from their dispossession of

25 See Tim Flannery, *The Future Eaters* and Bruce Pascoe's *Dark Emu.*

their land. The guilt we white inhabitants feel is sometimes overwhelming and has to be eliminated and jettisoned: it is too painful to acknowledge and absorb the truth of the cost of our prosperity and the damage done to the land as a result of it.

The denial of this truth can lead us to be in a 'frozen' and static/binary position of distancing ourselves from the past – 'what has that got to do with me' and 'why can't they just get over it?' are the questions we often hear. This is the split (Klein's paranoid-schizoid) position in evidence. If I, as a white person, am to think well of myself, then I must 'forget' the injustice that has occurred and blame the first inhabitants of this land for their failure to hold onto the land and for all their current troubles. Failing this, the emotional pendulum may swing the opposite way and I may be overwhelmed by guilt and think of myself as the bad one (the inheritor of violence and dispossession) and so I may see Aborigines as faultless and idealise their life before white settlement, seeing only good there.

Neither position is realistic. Both views are extremes of the desire to rid ourselves of grief over past trauma. But it is only in seeing both good and bad in self and other that a more congruent and complex response can emerge (Klein's so-called depressive position). It is a fantasy to believe that we have each made our successful lives on our own merits, alone. We have each made our lives according to the abilities we have and the opportunities we have been given and the support of others, including those who came before us. There is a direct link to the past in what we can achieve now. But the guilt of having achieved off the suffering of others is too hard to accept, so we deny the truth of it and we get caught in both blaming victims for their situation and in claiming any success as our own personal skill or hard work. Thus individualising is rewarded and reinforced in post-modern capitalism, as has been argued throughout this book and demonstrated yet again by our recent prime minister and prime ministers before him.

In 1997, the then Prime Minister John Howard, gave an apology to our First Nation Peoples as part of the opening of the first official Convention on Reconciliation. Readers may recall that in this apology John Howard distanced himself and people today from the atrocities that occurred in Australia's past. As indigenous audience members began to stand and turn their backs to the Prime Minister, in a gesture of not hearing, the Prime Minister deviated from prepared notes and defended government policies which had in all likelihood made the situation for current First Nations Peoples worse (Gooder & Jacobs 2000:230). The apology was neither heartfelt, nor appropriate and it was not accepted.

When an apology has an unspoken aim to triumph over a past, or has a sentiment of grievance, anger, guilt or regret at its heart, it is what Melanie Klein (1935/1975) calls 'manic reparation'. She says that manic reparation is the fantasy desire that the division being experienced should just go away. It is the belief that, by simply apologising, we can return to a place of oneness, to have the other stop complaining or to assuage the feeling of guilt for damage done. It is fantasy and therefore manic because the damage has in fact been done and the prior state can never return. Relationship with others is damaged by events and apology is only true when this brokenness is acknowledged.

Interestingly, the United Church of Canada made an apology to First Nation People's there in 1986, which was also not accepted and which in effect caused further trauma. The apology is reproduced below (as found in Greenberg 2012) to illustrate that, while it does acknowledge wrongdoing, it makes excuses for that wrongdoing (i.e. we didn't hear). There was no recognition of the ongoing suffering inflicted by the church over succeeding generations and finally the apology seeks forgiveness (we ask you to forgive us and walk together with us). There was no talk of reparation for the wrongs of the past (Greenberg 2012).

While other churches in Canada also apologised, the United Church 1986 apology was the only one not accepted. In 1998, the United Church of Canada tried again to speak an acceptable apology. In the second apology, the United Church did not shy away from naming the depth of the suffering it had caused and from unreservedly apologising. In particular, it stated that the victims of church programs were innocent (you did nothing wrong) and it promised to work so that nothing like the past atrocities could occur again. It sought forgiveness, not from the wronged people, but from God. I think John would tell me this is theologically correct: to ask for God's forgiveness and grace as reparation is made freely and without reserve. CMN's restorative justice research is also clear on this point: the perpetrator has no right to ask their victim for forgiveness. It is a gift that only the victim of injustice can bestow. With this understanding, asking for God's forgiveness only makes sense if the petitioner has accepted his/her complicity in injustice was also, and perhaps foremost, acknowledges an offence against God.

These apologies and the elements contained in them are reminiscent of the principle of restorative justice, as researched for CMN in 2008 and again in 2009 by Derek Brookes and as referred to earlier in this book.

United Church, Canada Apology to First Nations Peoples 1986

Long before my people journeyed to this land, your people were here, and you received from your Elders an understanding of creation and of the Mystery that surrounds us all that was deep, and rich, and to be treasured. We did not hear you when you shared your vision. In our zeal to tell you of the good news of Jesus Christ we were closed to the value of your spirituality. We confused Western ways and culture with the depth and breadth and length and height of the gospel of Christ.

We imposed our civilization as a condition for accepting the gospel. We tried to make you be like us and in so doing we helped to destroy the vision that made you what you were. As a result you, and we, are poorer and the image of the Creator in us is twisted, blurred, and we are not what we are meant by God to be.

We ask you to forgive us and to walk together with us in the Spirit of Christ so that our peoples may be blessed and God's creation healed.

United Church, Canada Residential Schools: 1998 Apology to First Nations

As Moderator of The United Church of Canada, I wish to speak the words that many people have wanted to hear for a very long time. On behalf of The United Church of Canada, I apologize for the pain and suffering that our church's involvement in the Indian Residential School system has caused. We are aware of some of the damage that this cruel and ill-conceived system of assimilation has perpetrated on Canada's First Nations peoples. For this we are truly and most humbly sorry.

To those individuals who were physically, sexually, and mentally abused as students of the Indian Residential Schools in which The United Church of Canada was involved, I offer you our most sincere apology. You did nothing wrong. You were and are the victims of evil acts that cannot under any circumstances be justified or excused.

We know that many within our church will still not understand why each of us must bear the scar, the blame for this horrendous period in Canadian history. But the truth is, we are the bearers of many blessings from our ancestors, and, therefore, we must also bear their burdens.

Our burdens include dishonouring the depths of the struggles of First Nations peoples and the richness of your gifts. We seek God's forgiveness and healing grace as we take steps toward building respectful, compassionate, and loving relationships with First Nations peoples.

We are in the midst of a long and painful journey as we reflect on the cries that we did not or would not hear, and how we have behaved as a church. As we travel this difficult road of repentance, reconciliation, and healing, we commit ourselves to work toward ensuring that we will never again use our power as a church to hurt others with attitudes of racial and spiritual superiority. We pray that you will hear the sincerity of our words today and that you will witness the living out of our apology in our actions in the future.

A true apology has several elements that make it authentic. The person apologising begins with an admission of wrongdoing and specifies the details of the hurt caused to demonstrate their level of understanding of the trauma (not to make excuses, but to say I see now what I put you through). The person takes responsibility for what happened. They express their regret and offer an apology: I am sorry. They say that it will not happen again and indicate future plans that demonstrate this intention.

Often those who apologise seek forgiveness from those they have wronged, but the aim of a true apology is not to beg for or force acceptance of the apology. That is not the purpose of a true apology. It will be up to the wronged parties to determine for themselves if the apology is accepted or not. But the first step is recognition and acknowledgment of the harm done by the person apologising.

In his now famous *Redfern Address*, Paul Keating, Prime Minister at an earlier time (1991-1996) came closer than John Howard to uttering a true apology.

It begins, I think, with that act of recognition. Recognition that it was we who did the dispossessing. We took the traditional lands and smashed the traditional way of life. We brought the diseases. The alcohol. We committed the murders. We took the children from their mothers. We practised discrimination and exclusion. It was our ignorance and our prejudice. And our failure to imagine these things being done to us. With some noble exceptions, we failed to make the most basic human response and enter into their hearts and minds. We failed to ask - how would I feel if this were done to me? As a consequence, we failed to see that what we were doing degraded all of us.[26]

---

26 Prime Minister Paul Keating, *Redfern Address* 1992 https://antar.org.au/sites/default/files/paul_keating_speech_transcript.pdf

We can only come to a position of true apology when we can walk in the shoes of the other, as Keating suggests. Apology is nothing without reparation. By reparation I mean repairing, mending, renewing or restoring relationships that have been damaged by previous bad behaviour. Reparation identifies, names and speaks the truth of suffering, loss, guilt and brokenness. True reparation acknowledges that it is not possible to return to the state of being prior to the loss or change. But it seeks to repair. The desire to repair comes from love and admiration of the harmed person so that guilt is experienced when we see that we have hurt or diminished the loved person in some way.

The psychoanalyst, Melanie Klein wrote about this idea of reparation. She said it is about love triumphing over hate and is part of the journey undertaken by us all as we mature. She said that apology and reparation come about when the person who has caused the injury realises their error and takes responsibility for the hurt inflicted. That person sees the damage that has been done and is perhaps shocked that they could have really inflicted this pain and at the same time realises that they do not want the other person to suffer.

True reparation requires love and regard for the injured party(ies) and the desire to repair, whereas 'manic reparation' is a personal defence against the guilt and shame of having caused harm. It is characterised by the desire to have the wronged person go away and stop complaining (because it calls to mind so painfully the wrong caused). It does not seek repair and is not coming from a place of love or esteem. It seems that true apology is hard for Australians to make towards indigenous peoples, perhaps because love and high regard of our first people is still unavailable to us, just as introspection and forgiveness of ourselves are also unavailable. Perhaps we are overinvested in the fantasy that we each are responsible for our own individual success in life.

In September 2018, the Prime Minister of Australia (Scott Morrison), tweeted about the sanctity of Australia Day with no apparent awareness of the hurt that his view might inflict on those who were dispossessed on that day. He said...indulgent self-loathing doesn't make Australia stronger. Being honest about our past does. Our modern Australian nation began on 26 January 1788....

The comment is interesting because it suggests that those who grieve for the loss of society and culture before white settlement are indulgent and that this is unhelpful if we are to make Australia stronger. The comment raises questions: is Australia weak? Does it need to be stronger? What makes it stronger? What is lost and gained in the desire to be strong? It seems that weak and strong are being put forth as binaries, with weak being bad and strong being good.

Further questions are raised by the comment about indulgence. The Prime Minister portrays indulgence as a negative state, as if indulgence is a weakness. Nevertheless, the dictionary defines indulgence as being liberal, tolerant, forgiving, merciful and humane. The word indulgence has come to mean a weak and negative disposition. This is an example of cultural hegemony whereby we come to believe the inverse of the true meaning of a word. But being merciful and tolerant is the path to reparation; it is one of the first steps in undertaking work that repairs the broken relationships of the past and can allow Australians to see they may be worthy of forgiveness by those whom white settlers have wronged, starting from 26 January 1788, but still continuing today.

It is in keeping with the prevailing ideology of post-modern capitalism that the Prime Minister would consider any form of guilt or regret of the past as self-loathing and therefore anathema. Embedded in his comment is the view that the way things are now is the best and only way they can be - life began in 1788 for Australia and 60,000 years of living before that mean nothing. Also encoded in the comment is the view that we must only look forward; the past is irrelevant and that Australia is on a trajectory of growth and forward momentum.

The Prime Minister's tweet perfectly encapsulates the 'frozen' and binary position that I have argued is not conducive to true reflection and deeper growth, but rather maintains the ideology of us/them. In contrast, Klein argues that if we can look, then it is possible that our guilt is not after all, endless. Apology and reparation are psychic work for individuals, but also, I think for colonised nations. John would say that we cannot be in right relationship with God, if we are not in right relationship with our neighbour (and ourselves). Without right relationships, we cannot prosper.

The disease of modernity – profit over people

The dominant discourse today is that of neoliberalism (also sometimes called economic rationality) where the emphasis is on the heroic individuality of humankind to tame, control and reap benefit from the environment. This ideation leads to the promotion of the concepts of entrepreneurship, flexibility and mobility. It encompasses the idea that humankind is on a linear trajectory to ever-greater heights of achievement and progress.

It is also characterised by the 'inevitable' uncovering of the secrets of life by science for the progress of humankind, the rejection of traditional and religious views and the ascension of the individual as the key, autonomous and self-determining factor in their own life. But rather than leading to enriched and empowered individual lives, John and I believe this ideology more often leads to short term contract work (Sennett 1998), a transactional view of relationship and loss of connectedness to organisations and community.

Modern life encapsulates a notion that capitalism is a progressive force and therefore inevitable. As Wood suggests (1997:543) *it treats specifically capitalist laws of motion as if they were the universal laws of history*, thus making capitalism historically invisible to us. We tend to speak of our particular economic order as if it were the best and the most progressive system. Some writers suggest that we are in a phase of post-capitalism, where capitalism is not merely the economic order, but where the notion of 'economic man' is seen as relevant, appropriate and correct for every aspect of human social activity. This notion is so pervasive that we do not see how its logic invades all aspects of our political and social lives.

The language of neoliberalism is now so dominant that we re-frame virtually all activities into the language of the market economy (Cummins 2002). The tenets of neoliberalism are so pervasive that we don't even question them. It is almost impossible to imagine another way of organising ourselves. We believe that we are autonomous individuals, that we are innately competitive, the market is the key way we interact, that it offers a free and level field of play for everyone and that we only ever get what we deserve through hard work.

But the truth is that capitalism is markedly increasing inequality around the world. Since 1980, the World Inequality Report has shown that there has been rising inequality occurring in most parts of the world.[27] Economic inequality is largely

---

27 https://theconversation.com/global-inequality-is-on-the-rise-but-at-vastly-different-rates-across-the-world-88976

driven by the unequal ownership of capital, which can be either privately or publicly owned. The *World Inequality Report*[28] shows that, since 1980, very large transfers of public to private wealth occurred in nearly all countries, whether western or developing. The richest 1% of people in the world now has as much wealth as the rest of the world combined, according to Oxfam and the richest 62 individuals in the world have more wealth than the bottom 50% of the poor in the world.[29]

Capitalism is a global phenomenon. For thirty or more years, we have witnessed a worldwide consensus around globalisation, deregulation and an increased focus on the importance of the private sector (Bridgman et al 2018). Capitalism is a universally aspirational system of not just economies, but whole cultures. Just look at the changes in China as a result of the movement from a rural economy to capitalism (in this case, state-sanctioned). A recent article in the *South China Morning Post*[30] quoted a Chinese billionaire as saying...*wealth creation is supported by government policies liberating the economy.* The same report says the number of individual billionaires in China grew from around 16 to 373 in the past twelve years. But how can China accept this level of wealth for the few, when thirty million live in poverty according to the Chinese government's own figures?[31]

Wealth for the few, with poverty and 'just managing' for the many is not a fair system. And China is one of the newer arrivals into the culture of profit. Note the language used by the Chinese billionaire that the economy is liberated. In other words, the ability to make this profit is free for him to exploit. But not for

---

28   https://wir2018.wid.world/
29   http:/bbc.com/news/business-35339475
30   https://scmp.com/news/world/united-states-canada/article/2170348/china-making-two-billionaires-every-week-worlds
31   http://xinhuanet.com/english/2018-02/01/c_136942195.htm

those who work under its yoke. The *Guardian*[32] newspaper has highlighted that little has changed at Foxconn where iphones are made in China and where in 2010, there were eighteen suicide attempts by workers (fourteen confirmed deaths). China is by no means unique in its race to make profit at the expense of people, their fruitful lives and their dignity. It is easier to see because it is a newer entrant into the race and its numbers of workers are so large as to command attention.

In 2011, CMN wrote a report using data from United Voice (the cleaners and hospitality workers union) about the lack of dignity afforded shopping centre cleaners, as cleaning companies cut the price of their tender bid every year in order to keep their cleaning contract. The large shopping centres in Australia use a system of tendering out their cleaning services. It is a very competitive arrangement. In order to win the tender and get the contract to do the cleaning, cleaning businesses bid, quoting lower prices each time a tender comes up (although of course the amount of work is the same or even greater). But who pays the price for this squeeze on cleaning contracts? It is not the shopping centres of this country, it is not the cleaning companies themselves; it is the worker who must still complete the cleaning tasks, but with either less pay or via shorter shifts. The work still has to be done, and the minimum pay is set nationally, so cleaners simply have to do their jobs taking longer unpaid hours or 'cut corners' (as the report is titled) to complete their work.

The United Voice website[33] notes that low rates of pay, underpayment, unpaid overtime, areas too large to clean, excessive workloads, inadequate equipment and having to

---

32 https://theguardian.com/technology/2017/jun/18/foxconn-life-death-forbidden-city-longhua-suicide-apple-iphone-brian-merchant-one-device-extract (extract from Brian Merchant book called The One Device)

33 The *Cutting Corners Report* can be found here https://unitedvoicevic.org.au/research

work through breaks are some of the injustices experienced by some shopping centre cleaning companies exposed through this research. But occupational health and safety must come before profit. These are moral issues as well as risk factors for work injury and work stress. We simply cannot allow the situation to continue whereby the safety we offer workers is the safety we can 'afford' without diminishing profit.

> *While low-paid work, compressed work schedules, and intensified work pressure are revealed as risk factors for work stress and work injury, and are clearly identified as occupational health and safety issues, they need to be understood also as moral issues. Poor work structures will violate cleaners' body, mind and spirit, and can then weigh them down as sufferers of injustice. This is an offence against the human dignity conferred upon each person, and needs to be redeemed.*
> (Bottomley &Neith 2011:28)

For John, theologically, this description of working conditions as an offence against human dignity is a description of evil. When human dignity is viewed as God-given, the wilful offence against it is an offence against God. It is an evil act bent on intentionally destroying God's good creation. So, capitalism is not a benign system and the best we can hope for; it is destructive of the earth and of the sense of the common humanity of people across the globe. In capitalism, self-interest is normalised, being vulnerable is weakness and therefore care for the vulnerable is also weakness, so, of course, it is low paid work.

But it does not have to be this way, as European countries attest. In an article by Max Roser in *The Guardian*, Roser provides data that shows that the gap is growing between rich and poor in UK, Canada, Australia, but not so in Germany, France, Holland, Denmark or Sweden, suggesting it is not inevitable and that government policies and taxation laws can reduce the imbalance.[34]

Democratically elected governments (and church entities) must regain control over the rampant profiteering that occurs today. The power of multinational companies is aptly demonstrated in the case of the filming of *The Hobbit* in New Zealand in 2010, but govenrments must not allow it. The USA company, Warner Bros., did not react well to an attempt by the actors' union to get better pay and conditions for its members working on the film. Warner Bros. simply threatened to make the movie elsewhere. This led to the New Zealand government agreeing to change its own labour laws, resulting in diminished employment rights for those who worked on the film and with no right of redress. In addition, the government gave Warner Bros. tax subsidies to stay and make the film in Wellington (Bridgeman et al 2018). Warner Bros. used its power and size to pressure the New Zealand government to abandon its laws which protected its own citizens from exploitation.

If we were to think of a 'perfect world' or of heaven on earth, would it have at its heart a system where some individuals use the work of others to make themselves rich? We speak as if there is no alternative to the economic system that puts private profit above the safety and dignity of people. John would argue that because we do not put God at the centre, we are caught in believing things to be true, which are not. We raise other things to the important place of God and we lose our humanity in the process. When citizens are merely commodities whose labour (physical or intellectual) is bought and sold, the intrinsic dignity

---

34 https://theguardian.com/news/datablog/2015/mar/27/income-inequality-rising-falling-worlds-richest-poorest

of the person (as a creation of God) is lost. We are worth far more than what our labour is valued in a marketplace.

The dignity of the person lost

The issue here is the conflict between the opportunities of a free market to make profit and the fundamental dignity of people at work. For John, this conflict is made clear when we look at occupational health and safety regimes. He says (Bottomley 2015:131)...

> When the truth about the place of death in life is not respected, then the culture itself becomes fragmented, confusing and often destructive. This is the culture of work. It is the culture that influences what level of occupational health and safety is affordable. It is the culture that influences what level of workers' compensation is affordable. It is a culture that places economic value at the centre of human affairs, and so dehumanises workers who are injured or die ...

These are stark words from John and they help us to see the truth of the situation; doing what is right is subordinate to making a profit. How language can be used to hide the truth about workplace safety is remarkable. We have 'incidents' and 'accidents' at work, where a worker may 'pass away' or a life is 'lost' (rather than die). But people die doing their work because profit comes first. We use language (often without realising it) to distance ourselves from the pain and fear of death and to pretend it is not ever present. The profound inability we each have to control what might happen to us over the course of our lifetime and also in the manner of our death is hidden and avoided in this speech. The psychologist, Winnicott (1975) reminds us that liveliness is only real when deadness is acknowledged. As concepts, they go together.

The language of the market has infected the language we use to go about our daily lives and it is used to maintain the lie that capitalism brings wealth and prosperity and to distance us from those who fail, fall through the cracks, or who are weak. The liveliness associated with business language is false when the goal is to be always changing and improving without acknowledgment of loss, pain and death. When the terms used to describe successful businesses are analysed, an irrational desire to avoid deadness is apparent – just think about it: driving change, continuous improvement, moving forward, accelerated change, growing the business, in the pipeline, on the runway, fast tracking. Countless business terms are associated with rapid and indeed constant movement. It is not rational to expect any enterprise to be constantly in a state of rapid forward movement and yet we are all caught up in it. One of Facebook's values (is it a value?) is "move fast" and for Google, one value is "fast is better than slow" while another is "great is just not good enough".

Let's take a moment to think if these buzzwords (I couldn't call them values) are healthy and desirable? I don't really want to be on the treadmill of continuous improvement. Sure, I want to do my best and yes, I understand that we need some way to measure if we are doing well for our clients or customers. But can everything in life be measured? The Australian four biggest banks have been preoccupied with 'winning back trust' following the revelations of the Financial Services Royal Commission. Trust is not 'winnable'. It is a gift of the other, the same as forgiveness. And I also want to be able to acknowledge that I have some good days at work and some where I don't achieve much at all – for a variety of reasons, some of which are opaque to me.

I like to reflect on why that might occur. I prefer to think about the relationships I have that may be damaged by inattention. I want to sit in stillness for a while and wonder if what I am doing is actually worthwhile in itself. I want to ponder taking another path and I wish I were encouraged to look at each issue in a complex, connective and systemic way at work. But should I be continuously improving? It is possible? Is it desirable? It reminds me of the linear progress myth in action again. We speak as if we are on a journey ever upward to a better and brighter future. But most often under capitalism, the way forward is simply more and more profit for the few: it is not about better relationships, fairness, equality or the dignity of humanity. It is simply about money. And not-for-profit agencies are not immune to this infection. For them it is about seeing more clients, getting more government grants or bequests, proving with outcome measures that they are worthy of receiving yet more funding and sometimes bullying staff into working harder (and so often for lower pay) because of the good cause they labour for.

But wherever we work, sadly, we are labouring to prop up an unfair and unjust system. It is worth noting that one of the first issues unions raised with John at the Church and Trade Unions Committee in the late 1980s was the exploitation of their members working in church-run community services agencies and I had a similar experience working for the Brotherhood of St Laurence in the mid-1980s. The organisation had lost money on the stock exchange (we were told) and as a consequence the lowest paid staff needed to give up their long-standing agreement of a 35-hour week and work longer hours for the same pay to compensate for this stock market loss. So the lowest paid, were required to pay for unsuccessful stock market speculation at the Brotherhood of St Laurence. Economic growth becomes an imperative that narrows life to the service of this goal. But by narrowing life to the attainment of economic goals, violence and injustice can easily be done to those under its yoke. It is no wonder that only 13% of us feel engaged at work, worldwide.[35]

There is enormous pressure to believe the hype that we must continually improve and the requirement to demonstrate it at work is enormous and it leads to anxiety and stress. I observe this as I consult to organisations and work with 'dysfunctional' teams and when I am asked to 'coach' underperforming staff. The dysfunction and underperformance I witness is generally scapegoating of a person or team for the failure of the organisation itself to live its own professed values. Some staff take it to heart that the organisation they work for is not 'practising what it preaches'. They find that this contradiction strips them of energy and incentive.

All businesses these days have values statements; many have up to ten 'core' values (I always wonder what the non-core values are and about their unspoken impact) and frequently behaviours are specified that must explicitly match these values, with staff measured and tested on compliance with them. Typically words such as integrity, compassion, respect, innovation, honesty, courage and justice are used in value statements as rallying cries to staff to do better and keep improving. One of the first people to present to UMN's injured workers group in the mid-1980s was an office worker from a trade union suffering a repetition strain injury and bullying from her manager for failing to keep up the office's productivity.

In my consulting experience, the contradiction between the values of the organisation and the behaviour that actually occurs is generally what causes dysfunction and underperformance. People cannot work effectively when they are required to behave only in sanctioned ways and punished (by being ostracised

35 https://news.gallup.com/poll/165269/worldwide-employees-engaged-work. aspx

generally) if they do not. While at the same time, they do not see this behaviour modelled by others in the organisation. In organisations I have consulted to, I have found this contradiction alive and well (although denied) when I am brought in to solve the problem. The solution is often already given to me in advance. The senior leader who contracts with me asks me to choose a new leader for the team or help the underperforming staff member to leave the organisation. I am generally brought in too late, after much damage has already been done to the dignity of a member of staff or a team. Institutional violence is hidden under the banner of work ideology – we all have to be more efficient. Anyone who can't cope with that prevailing view is told in one way or the other that this is their own individual problem.

In his work with Palliative Care Victoria (Bottomley & Tehan 2002), John interviewed thirty people with his colleague, Mary Tehan, including 10 with life-threatening illnesses, their work colleagues, bosses and carers. What he found was that those who were ill found that working had given them independence and a sense of worth. With illness, this is taken away. People become (in their own words) dependent, a burden, defined as the illness and nothing more. John commented that they lived with the dominant narrative about what makes a person valuable – that is hard work and according to that measure, they fail. Their illness means they can feel isolated and can be seen as discredited, restricted and burdensome.

In our current economic system, the value of a life is reduced to the economics of the cost of replacing the worker (as if the person were a part in a machine). The payout to family for workplace death or injury is mandated to a maximum amount and is based on the reduced earning capacity of the injured person. There are tables available on the internet that list the payout for injuries and death. Loss of an index finger in a work accident will get the injured up to $54,000 payout. Loss of fertility will get you less than $50,000, while complete paraplegia is worth just under $300,000.[36] You may argue that, of course, we need a guide for these unfortunate instances, and that is true, but the guide is based on the most basic assumption of the value of a life: likely future income. John says that it is 'spiritual blindness' to equate the dignity of human life to amount of money that can be earned by an individual.

The ideology of work promises that the meaning and worth of your life will be gifted to you in return for your devotion to the idol of hard work...[T]he promise of the 'good life' held out by hard work has produced such spiritual blindness in Australia that God's warning about the bitter fruit of this misplaced trust has been forgotten (Bottomley 2015:142)

Binary notions

John speaks of the separation of Word and deed in Christian churches and the banishing of emotion and faith to the private sphere, while the public sphere carries on as if progress, growth, rationality, the economy are all leading us to perfection. He argues that by locating 'fact' in the rational public world of the economy, any emotion or belief can be only spoken of in terms of home and family and is seen to have no wider societal consequence.

Our modern times seem to foster many binaries: abundance/scarcity, public/private, rational/emotional, rich/

---

36 https://www.worksafe.qld.gov.au/__data/assets/pdf_file/0004/88231/table-of-injuries-for-injuries-on-or-after-2-november-2005-to-14-october-2013.pdf

poor, competitive/cooperative and us/them. Binaries make complex situations feel simple and easy to grasp. We can believe that emotion is something to be controlled, that it is personal and private. We can act competitively at work, because that is how we are 'supposed' to be. But binaries stunt our growth and development as fully human. They do not allow Hegelian dialectic to undercover new knowledge from deep exploration of profound and contradictory ideas. They do not encourage us to see our own failure and the grace inherent in embracing failure, asking for forgiveness and in seeking justice. They cause us to split good from bad and view opinion as if it were fact.

The evidence of the pain and grief of individuals who have suffered injustice at work is removed from discourse in the public realm. It effectively becomes invisible and those who suffer injustice are made voiceless. But as a minister of religion, John is also clear that voices that express a view counter to the prevailing regime embody the suffering of Christ and need to be heard. He is very strong in his view that the splitting and denigration of faith and emotion from science and rationality is leading us to a path of destruction. He sees the church as complicit in this polarity. He suggests that the church prays now to...

A domesticated God consigned to the private sphere of life – to home, its localised geography and leisure (or non-work) time – where all that is required of God is a blessing for the humanly ordained structures of injustice...(Wallace & Bottomley 2012:87)

Another binary is that of scarcity and abundance. The faith view is that abundance is everywhere around us, due to God's goodness in creation. But as noted earlier, capitalism functions on the notion of scarcity. It is what allows a price to be put on commodities. In capitalist workplaces, we are out of practice with giving and sharing without counting the cost and we focus on the fears raised by this model of competition for scarce resources.

The belief in the scarcity of all good things in the economic sense has invaded all areas of life and leads us to see scarcity everywhere. The fear of lack of resources (both external and internal) can trigger the desire to gather and hoard. The problem with this focus on scarcity is that it can lead us to fear, denigrate and persecute 'the other'. We may come to believe, for example, there is not enough room for refugees in Australia, or that those needing government benefits are "bludgers". If we believe this view is correct and is shared by many in our society, then we can disparage others if they do not fit our view.

There is so much talk of values these days, it seems to me they arise in inverse proportion to the enactment of real values in our lives. So, business makes more profit, but hides this fact by naming its values. The values of the Commonwealth Bank are integrity, collaboration, excellence, accountability and service. After the Banking Royal Commission, it is no wonder there is cynicism around values. The talk about values feels empty to me, as if we have lost any way to speak meaningfully about the value and purpose of life. Since faith is consigned to the private realm of personal belief, there is no overarching system of values to inform us and capitalism's only value, seems to be profit. I don't feel there is any consensus or depth when we discuss values: it is just what each of us individually wants the value words to mean. The appeal to values is heard in politics too.

What are these Australian values that we hear so often in politicians' speeches? The first speech as Prime Minister given by Scott Morrison in 2018 was littered with talk of values, few of which were explicated. It was not clear how any of them could be called uniquely Australian values. For example, the Prime Minister[37] says ...*we've all got to live by the rules of this country, the law of our land. These are values we uphold.* And again...*we believe in choice. And because of that, it means we believe in our future.* Our own Prime Minister struggles to elucidate values that Australians can live by – values that allow our full humanity to flourish.

Underneath his rhetoric we can dimly see the Adam Smith notion of the inevitability of positive progress (believe in the future), the 'truth' of the self-interested, autonomous individual who controls his/her destiny (believe in choice) and the social contract that is entered to keep the system in place (we've got to live by the rules of this country). How can 'believing in the future' be called a value? And how do we believe in the future, anyway? Apparently, it is a future for everyone, but in reality it is only for those who work hard, as evidenced in this quote from the same speech.

There is a fair go for those who have a go. That is what fairness in Australia means.

This is another example of reification of the tired binary of 'hard work' and success. Scott Morrison joins a long line of Prime Ministers who are captive to this ideology. Is it the role of PMs to support the cultural hegemony of the status quo? For me, 'a fair go' means equality of access and opportunity regardless of who you may be or where you came from or how hard you work or how lucky you have been in your life. It is about community and relationships, regardless. How much of a 'fair go' are those who cannot find work getting? Or homeless people? Or asylum seekers, when the government has opposed legislation to allow sick refugees who are in offshore detention facilities the right to be evacuated for medical treatment.

---

37 https://www.afr.com/news/transcript-of-new-prime-minister-scott-morrisons-first-press-conference-20180824-h14h1a

Everything in capitalism has a value placed on it and items that are scarce, but in demand can command higher prices. The default position, therefore, inside a capitalist market economy is to attach a price to everything and to argue that the thing we are selling is indeed scarce. In a competitive environment, we tend to think of everything as a resource that is owned and can be bought and sold. This includes intellectual resources and labour and in capitalism; we see resources as scarce.

Smith (2003) argues that scarcity is a concept that assists capitalism to operate, but it is a collective belief, a shared presumption, which we have absorbed under capitalism, rather than a truth. This is the way capitalism works. We cannot make money from things that are freely available and in abundance. Since in capitalism there is a price on everything, then everything is measured as having more or less value according to the desire of consumers to buy it and the relative scarcity of obtaining the object.

The problems we face today are not those of scarcity – the earth is, of course, still abundant – the issue is about how resources are distributed to the benefit of all and to secure the future of the earth.

the conditions of seeming scarcity that rule our lives, fill us with anxiety, and keep us on unproductive treadmills, result primarily from our way of thinking and not from the natural order of things (Smith 2003:483)

I have noted the continual forward motion apparent in capitalism: growth at any cost! I mentioned earlier the desire to keep moving to avoid any sense of 'deadness' and the church's tacit agreement with this view. The UCA Synod of Victoria and Tasmania's response to the disaster of debt following the failure of Acacia College is an example: the Synod's 'recovery' program proceeded under the mantra of 'Uniting our Future', a name that hid and denied the deep pain that may still simmer across the church, as properties were sold to cover the debt.

Continual economic growth may help us to avoid the fear of death, but it will lead eventually to the death of our planet. These binaries are everywhere in our language and supported by those with power in our capitalist economy to maintain the status quo. Whether this happens consciously or sometimes unconsciously is unclear. In an example of the polarities existing today, the Hungarian Prime Minister[38] in answering a journalist's question on tolerance of gay rights in Hungary betrayed the typical binaries inherent in the political system today;

Hungary is a tolerant nation. Tolerance, however, does not mean that we would apply the same rules for people whose lifestyle is different from our own. We differentiate between them and us.

The splitting of 'us' from 'them' is a hallmark of capitalist economies. John speaks of the language used in health and safety at work as demonstrative of the way we hide the truth of the damage done to people at work. Often, actions at work that inflict injury are called 'incidents' and an employer may be found guilty of 'misconduct' and fined when someone has in fact died at work. Using a word such as 'misconduct' hides the power relations at work.

The use of language is significant: the banking royal commission was (when finally agreed by the government) into *misconduct*, whereas the politically motivated royal commission into unions – covered governance and *corruption*. The 'misconduct' of the banks has been exposed, following the royal commission,

---

38 https://hrj.leeds.ac.uk/2018/10/28/billy-elliot-in-hungary-orban-and-tolerance/

not merely as misconduct, but as significant corruption with greed at its heart. But will anyone be gaoled for this corruption? Employers rarely go to gaol for murder or manslaughter.

In 2017, the union movement revived its 2004 campaign for the introduction of industrial manslaughter laws. This followed the successful campaign in other states spurred on by the community outcry over a spate of shocking deaths in their own jurisdictions. The law is already in place in Queensland and the Australian Capital Territory and operates in the UK (Naismith 2017:4). Grief experienced by family members after a loved one's preventable workplace death is more than private grief at the loss of a loved one, it is also a lament that names what is unjust in the structure and beliefs of the modern world. But there are few opportunities for this lament to be made public. It is quietly dealt with in courts and in monetary settlements. The grief accompanying an unjust death is complex and cries out for public acknowledgment, not simply being dismissed as private angst. John and colleagues have created opportunities through public memorials sponsored by support groups for families bereaved by work-related deaths, such as Gippsland Asbestos-related Diseases Support and the CMN's GriefWorks program. These public memorials and public events call out injustice.

In the prophetic tradition, lament voiced to God's mercy is located squarely in the public world. Such lament is never shut away by the claims of other powers or belief systems. Such grief is a protest against the dehumanising ideology of work (Bottomley 2015:30)

In order to critique the binaries of modern capitalism, we need to take the time to question if what we think we know is actually correct. Is emotion truly separate from fact? Is reason somehow superior to emotion? Is it a good thing to keep personal and family life separate from work life? (Can it even be done successfully?). Is the earth abundant? Relegation of emotion to the private sphere AND the "rightness" of the current system means that individuals who don't succeed are blamed. It is considered an individual pathology, not a systemic failure. But if we think carefully, we do know that work is not all there is to life; it is not the meaning of life. While work may be enjoyable and rewarding for some, in fact for many it is 'soul destroying' labour and we know that there is no 'level playing field' in our society, where everyone gets a fair go.

As I noted in chapter two, the German philosopher Georg Hegel investigated 'how we know what we think we know' and theorised new ways of looking at how knowledge and understanding are discovered and understood. Hegel spoke of the 'phenomenology of mind' where he argued (in a rather more complex manner than described here) that a mind comes to know itself and understand the world by a successive integration of ideas and sense impressions. It moves on its path to true knowledge and understanding by first experiencing the world and itself, then acknowledging the contradictory movement of consciousness and ideas, dissolving and reforming in a dialectical movement. It sees that forms (ideas, objects or the impression of others) are not in fact as stable and as fixed as first thought. This is remarkably similar to the psychology of mind expounded by Klein.

Klein speaks of the development of mind, first with a rigid sense of good and bad and which later moves to a more nuanced understanding of each of us being both good and bad. This more nuanced understanding of self and the other comes about due to repeated interaction with others. Just as Klein noted the way the infant learns to distinguish between herself and other objects and people by repeated interaction, so Hegel also speaks of the gaining of knowledge by a complex interplay or dialogue between consciousnesses.

Similarly, John Bottomley expounds the grace of failure, loss, powerlessness and grief to remind us of the complexity of our human nature and to provide an opportunity to reconnect in our relationship with God. While they all look at matters from different standpoints, they discuss this complex interplay between minds, which lies at the heart of learning, and understanding. They abhor the polarising of thought and ideas into one extreme or the other. They see the path to maturity as the ability to see a point of view from the other person's perspective, to listen carefully to their way of seeing things, to incorporate their view, to see how it compares with their own ideas and then to creatively consider a new, more complex notion arising from this experience.

Similarly, Freud introduced the idea of the unconscious, where all unpleasant and unacceptable feelings, thoughts and urges rest (generally unknown and unavailable to us). Similarly, the way Wilfred Bion (following Melanie Klein) described it, some sensory perceptions are too disturbing for us to absorb and 'digest' and we try to expel them – we cannot tolerate them, believe them or accept the reality of them. Bion was thinking in particular here of fears and hatreds or guilt and shame. It is very hard to accept or absorb difficult emotions without repeated experience of feeling them in a safe way. For Bion (1962), this is called 'containment'. In relationship with trusted and reliable others, we learn to contain difficult and complex emotional material. We learn to accept the 'both/and' aspects of our humanity, rather than the 'either/or' viewpoint. (The reader will recall Klein calls the either/or position - splitting.) The split of emotion from reason and the belief in the dominance of reason leads to the effort to banish and deny emotions and their impact.

If we were to apply philosophical or psychoanalytic ideas to the system of capitalism in which we are enmeshed today, we might say that this system does not help or encourage each of us to digest complex emotional material, nor does it have room for a slow and deep exchange of ideas, it generally does not support the complex interplay of relationships (except as commodity exchange) and it does not help us to contain and accept contradictory sensations.

Marx and later left thinkers argued that the oversimplified way of looking at the world inherent in capitalism is because the 'ruling classes' wish to maintain their position and so they control not only the physical tools of economic production, but they develop complex means of convincing us of the absolute rightness of their way of seeing things. This is 'cultural hegemony' as described by Gramsci and it is characterised by simple binary notions, such as winners/losers, us/them, private/public, the truth/fake news, emotion/reason, moving fast/death, cooperative/competitive, rich/poor and scarcity/abundance.

We don't have to look far to see examples of these over-simplified and self-serving justifications, if we care to look. For example, when calls for wage justice are called 'the politics of envy', calls for equity and fairness are characterised as resentment and thereby dismissed as not legitimate. Efforts by historians to improve our knowledge of past atrocities are dismissed as untrue and labelled by politicians, including a Prime Minister (John Howard) as the 'black arm band view of history', which *belittles past achievements... encourages a 'guilt industry' and impedes rational thinking on current problems.*[39]

In Australia, the matter of refugees seems to be a spark for these binary notions. A recent academic journal article, (Crawley

---

39 https://www.aph.gov.au/About_Parliament/Parliamentary_Departments/
   Parliamentary_Library/pubs/rp/RP9798/98RP05

& Skleparis 2017:48) challenges what they call 'categorical fetishism', arguing that the dominant categories of naming refugees do not *capture adequately the complex relationship between political, social and economic drivers of migration or their shifting significance for individuals over time and space.* I certainly do not blame anyone for falling prey to this simplistic and polarising view of the world, as it is so pervasive that it is almost invisible to us. (In my efforts to raise the matter here, I may be guilty of polarising the argument, too). It is an all-encompassing way of thinking that is indiscernible to us. But if we can take the time to look more carefully it can be seen that it is merely a belief that humanity is entirely self-interested, rational, logical and that we are all working hard to progress towards an even better world in a linear path. It is just a belief; it is not necessarily fact. And the world exists with a myriad of beliefs existing side-by-side.

The hegemony of modernity provides the cultural foundations for capitalism to exist with belief in God now consigned to the private realm. And while there are benefits to following the belief of modernity that we are all free, self-interested and rational – it gives us hope, allows us to strive, gives us energy to fight and win; it has a significant cost too. It is the cost to relationships with others and thereby to learning by that interaction. It leads to a loss of connection with humanity generally, animals and the earth. It allows us to dispense with painful, difficult truths about the way we live our lives. It stunts our growth for compassion, relationship and meaningful dialogue.

For John, Christ's crucifixion is removed from the public sphere and seen as simply a private belief, but this positioning in the private realm is a deliberate attempt to limit the power of the death and resurrection of Christ to unmask the unjust abuse of imperial power. So the resurrection is minimised as a matter of private belief, and an ideological/hegemonic barrier is raised to weaken the power of God's love to transform death and renew life.

The orthodoxy of self-interest

At the heart of John's work are two key words – relationship and connection. This contrasts with the orthodox view, which sees humanity as essentially competitive and self-interested. The polarities described above keep us in a fixed state of apprehension and unable to see or believe any other way to organise ourselves. Perhaps Gramsci was right and we are all caught inside a culture that convinces us that no other way is possible. It seems hard to contradict the notion of self-interest, when we clearly see examples of it everywhere.

This is evident in the Royal Commissions Australia has had in recent times. There have been six Royal Commissions in the past five years (136 in total since Federation in 1901) and while two could be argued to be political motivated (Trade Unions and the Home Insulation Program), the other four were into aged care, child protection and youth detention in Northern Territory, institutional child abuse and, most recently, misconduct in the banking and finance sector. These Royal Commissions found widespread neglect, abuse, criminal behaviour, apathy, greed and wholesale disregard for the dignity of people in vulnerable situations. When people are thought of as commodities, they can be dismissed and abused more easily than if we uphold the dignity of each and every person and see them as our neighbours and fellow travellers.

While putting profit before relationships may lead inevitably to the loss of dignity for people, as John contends, it is also clear that in order to live and support ourselves, we do have to earn a living within the system. When I undertake consulting work with people who work for profit-making businesses, they usually give very little thought to questioning the way things are: they simply shrug and tell me that is just how it is and things can't be changed. Mostly, they put little effort into thinking about these weighty questions. They want to get ahead and do not question whether the system is fair.

But they are easy to work with as they are not burdened with guilt or shame and they eagerly embrace new ways of doing things at work. They have an energy and enthusiasm that is infectious. A belief in one's own autonomy and in working hard to get ahead does lead to the release of energy and positive action. In the non-for-profit sector, on the other hand, I have learned that staff who work in these agencies often have a more complex view of the world. They feel a clash with how things ought to be and how they are. They are much more complex and difficult to work with. They most often say to me that what I suggest won't work. Hope and energy are less obvious and pessimism is common.

So - is self-interest really all we are? I don't think so. I think we are capable of great empathy and selfless acts of bravery and stoicism. We are self-interested and so much more than that. But trust, support, relationship and companionship are 'commodities' in short supply in our capitalist system. I think this is so because it makes it easier to buy and sell at a profit if we do not build a close relationship with the other, then we do not come close to seeing the damage done by the greed inherent in the transaction. The only way, really to exploit people for profit is to not know them, not see them, not believe they have rights, believe they are gullible and therefore deserve what they get or believe they are not as human as us.

There are many basic narratives we can call on to avoid the guilt of prospering at the expense of another. It is my view that it is in relationship and connection that we each grow and learn, but it simultaneously opens us to our own fears, shame and guilt. So it is not an easy road. It is in connection that we prosper, not in competition. John sees that all of God's creation is connected and inter-related. There is a wholeness to this view that rejects the hegemonic culture's assigning of fear, shame and guilt to the private sphere, where they are judged by public rationality to be pathological.

John finds in his discovery of Ignatian spirituality a liberating wisdom that states that feelings of fear, guilt, shame and failure are not pathological but are also part of God's good creation. Similarly the practice of dadirri has allowed John to accept these feelings at times when they arise (perhaps with some struggle and the support of a spiritual director, or a professional practice supervisor, or the support of a good friend over lunch), and to discern God's calling from fear to new truths, from shame to new political possibilities, and from guilt to deeper personal responsibility. He believes things go horribly wrong when we assume or believe that we are each autonomous individuals forging our own paths without reference to, or understanding of, our connections with each other, with history, with the earth and with God at the centre of this connectivity.

Without God at the centre, systems such as ours can lead to anomie, the term quoted earlier (Durkheim). Similar in essence to the term anomie is *Alienation*. Karl Marx used the term to describe a situation in capitalism whereby our own labour comes to rule us, instead of a situation where we work and directly access the fruit of our labour, our labour becomes a commodity that is worth something in a market. In circumstances of alienation, human beings are only worth the value of our skills. Relationships are defined in economic terms, and not social terms and we are ruled by the value of our work. People become commodities that are traded (Marx called this commodity fetishism).

It seems to me that this describes the situation we have at present. So, while it is not popular to speak of Marx or to even think that we could organise ourselves socially in any way other than capitalism, more than 170 years ago, Karl Marx saw the potential for a society built on capitalism to be corrosive of social bonds. Sometimes concepts such as anomie or alienation are used in sociology to describe states of extreme loneliness and isolation - focusing on the individual and their separation from others. But this definition misses the key context in which the terms were originally situated. For both Durkheim and Marx respectively, the terms were about the inversion of connection in society, either by a breakdown of right relationships or abuse of power. They are the result of a corrupt society and they expose the failure of the social contract when they appear. Alienation does not refer to the individual failure to conform to a social system, but rather the failure of a social system to adequately support (morally, socially and economically) all its members. When I speak of Marx's concept of alienation with John, he speaks of the power of God's judgment when God's people turn away from God. So, for Marx the increase in alienation in a corrupt society should lead to its eventual downfall, whereas John might argue that God's judgment is invoked to terrible consequences by this corruption.

I sometimes wish I had John's certainty about what God wants for us. More often than not, I feel confused and frustrated by the way the world is and I feel powerless to improve it. But either way, I do think it is right that complexity, contradiction and the interplay of emotion and reason are really the authentic truth of humanity and that we learn by staying at the edge of certainty in collaboration with others who are different from ourselves.

In a very interesting book called *All that is Solid Melts into Air*, the author Marshall Berman (1982:35) quotes a Mexican poet, Octavio Paz, who says that our modern time is

> *... cut off from the past and continually hurtling forward at such a dizzy pace that it cannot take root, that it merely survives from one day to the next: it is unable to return to its beginnings and thus recover its powers of renewal.*

This quote highlights for me the fact that we are in an 'iron cage' as Max Weber (1905/1958) suggested; we do suffer alienation; we cannot see any other possibility to organise ourselves than with rationality governing everything we do as we forge ahead to a perfect future with capitalism as the supposedly best system of social arrangement. We rush everywhere, being busy at all times and fail to see clearly, to deeply listen, to slow down and wonder how else things might be. For Weber, the rise of capitalism and the rigid bureaucratic structures that accompany it mean that social connections become based on efficiency and individual gain, rather than a sense of connection and brotherhood, with the desire for wealth at the heart of the malaise.

> *The Puritan wanted to work in a calling; we are forced to do so...the care for external goods should only lie on the shoulders of the 'saint like a light cloak, which can be thrown aside at any moment.' But fate decreed that the cloak should become an iron cage.* (Weber 1905/1958:181)

Later translations of Weber's work have called the iron cage a 'steel hard shell', but the metaphor remains a powerful one. If we look only to the accumulation of external 'things' in efficient and transactional ways, we no longer see our work as a calling, as it was in religious days, but as a means of amassing wealth and prestige – or, more often, of simply surviving in a system that curbs freedom of expression.

As a university lecturer, I am acutely aware of this. The emphasis nowadays in the academy is on offering studies, which are attractive to students, so they can get ahead at work. The historic role of the university as the place of critical thinking and of discovering way of 'doing things differently' is undermined. John's work tries to address these critical failures with his integration of research, reflection, study, ritual and story-telling.

Since the rise of the Enlightenment, when religious faith fell out of favour and the material view of the world dominated, we have struggled with this lack of connection and with idolatry. John says idolatry is putting something that is not God in the place belonging to God. We put other things in the place that previously God occupied. Most often, the object put in the central place previously occupied by God is money – or more specifically the pursuit of material wealth. But I believe that we also put the notion of the autonomous, self-actualising individual in this central place. Self-interest is orthodoxy; it is assumed to be correct. The agency of the individual is at the forefront of our thinking in the modern era. We believe that we are all individually responsible for whatever success we make of life and this is most often measured by our material wealth. The language of the market economy dominates our language, our culture and permeates our way of thinking.

This view can be seen in the way we treat grieving people, as another example. It is as if their grief is individual and internal and they must work through it in a simple, linear fashion, in order to be re-integrated into work and society. If a person struggles with this or takes longer than is considered reasonable, then it is their individual failure (they didn't work hard enough) and systems and structures reinforce this view so that we do not have to look at the moral bankruptcy at the heart of our economic and individualistic system.

In Australia today, we are able to access ten subsidised sessions with a professional psychologist if needed to recover from a period of grief or depression and this is a terrific initiative of the government. The government offers sixteen sessions for 'complex grief'. But the system expects us to get over grief and return to 'normal' within that time frame. We need to be ever more efficient and effective in our lives and our work and so we measure as much as possible to demonstrate and benchmark our success.

If we fail, it is presumed by the system (and often ourselves) that we were (individually) not good enough or didn't work hard enough. Grief and its expression are somehow fearful and not really acceptable at work. In fact, any emotional problems are largely 'outsourced' these days with EAPs (employee assistance programs) where emotion is external to business and located firmly in individual pathology and outsourced to clinical psychology settings. The ideology of work quarantines death and grief from public life. The desire for progress and the belief in a form of linear progress is at the heart of this view. There is no acknowledgment that, say, continuous improvement may well be unattainable, irrational and, perhaps, persecutory for those under its yoke. Not to mention the impact of it on our environment.

But John's writing has countless examples of people for whom grief is unrelenting and for whom an unjust death has inter-generational consequences. Here is just one example from Maria, a woman John interviewed....

Bob hanged himself at the factory...the doctor put me on medication for depression and this made it difficult to be a single parent...over time, my daughter Kylie came to believe that in some way she was responsible for her father's death. In her teens, she began to drink heavily and to take drugs... eventually Kylie took a fatal overdose. I guess the fact that the doctor prescribed medication for me to cope was a message to my children that this was how people coped. (Bottomley 2015:111)

This vignette from Maria shows the long-term effect of death on a family, not to mention the workmates who found Bob's body at the factory. Maria's grief was medicalised and she was diagnosed with depression. In keeping with the prevailing business ideology of our time, the dominant view of grief is that it is (or perhaps that it 'should' be) private, individual and time limited. But this story demonstrates that it is not, and how could it be, given Maria's testimony?

John describes another story (Bottomley 2015:38) from Mary who was off work for over twelve months from a serious repetitive strain injury. She began to feel hopeless and worthless. Mary had internalised the idea that work makes us whole and successful. She felt a personal failure because her work caused her to become injured. Despite our belief in the separation of public and private, Mary's work injury and her subsequent emotional suffering invaded her home and family. She began to feel a burden on her family, as she could no longer 'pay her way'. This in turn affected her family members so much so that Mary's daughter had a breakdown, became suicidal and was in the care of a psychiatrist. In turn, Mary felt a failure as a mother to have been the cause of her daughter's illness.

The prevailing ideology would suggest that Mary is lacking resilience and her family members are 'weak of character'. But how would anyone react to a situation where their personal experience exposes the lie of capitalism that we are all simply self-interested and by our work we garner success and praise? Mary and her family had to live with the competing and contradictory views of the world and to question how her experience had shaped her identity.

These two stories demonstrate that we see ourselves as either winners or losers and that this thinking is so ingrained that it becomes almost impossible to live when something happens that shows us that no matter how good we are, how hard we work, things can go wrong for us and our sense of self and how we fit into society are shaken to the core.

When Maria and Mary's belief in the taken-for-granted reality of their world was shaken to the core, it seemed the only path left for their survival was the path to mental illness, where at last they found the 'comfort' of modern medicine. The theory of cognitive dissonance in psychology suggests that when there is an inconsistency between attitudes, beliefs or behaviours (dissonance), something must change to eliminate the dissonance. If two opposing worldviews collide and cannot be made consistent, then the inner world of the psyche collapses from the struggle to bring a consistency to beliefs and actions. Their pain was anesthetised, and the profound injustice their experience should have revealed was hidden from public view in the private space of their individual and family lives.

For John, telling Maria and Mary's stories is truth-telling, because just as miners would lower a canary into a coal mine to test the toxicity of the air, so these two women's stories tell us about the poisonous nature of injustice and unrighteousness stemming from modern beliefs and practices about the supposed redemptive quality of modern work. These women embody a prophetic judgment against the sinful and evil structures, practices, and beliefs about the work that is demanded of us in today's capitalist system. John's story-telling as truth-telling seeks to stand in the Amos tradition of prophetic justice to lament before God and our neighbour the injustice and harm that is done too often in God's name. Perhaps you know this prophetic voice: 'how long, O Lord, must people suffer from this abandonment of your justice?'

Inability to think (reification, ideology and hegemony)

The examples of the struggles of both Mary and Maria marry their own experience of failure with the expectations of our modern culture, remind me of the work of Wilfred Bion. He spoke of the desire in all of us as we mature to know and be known by others and he called this "K". It is how thinking and understanding develops for Bion, it is how we learn in relationship to others and has resonances with Hegel and Klein as described above. But in situations of fear and anxiety, K is hard to hold and Bion (1961) describes the lengths that we will go to (unconsciously) to defend ourselves from any knowledge that brings psychic pain. So for Bion, the clash of independently experienced views that are incompatible, can result in what he terms "–K" which means the inability to know; the active desire to be not known, where one is left in a fearful state with only a denuding of knowledge and understanding. For Bion, this state brings on mental illness.

John does not use the term 'the inability to think'; that is my interpretation, but he uses ideas that are similar to those I have learned from psychoanalytic and political theory. When a way of being in the world is manifestly unsustainable, corrupt and unfair, yet pervasive and the only way to survive is to embrace it, then we become trapped in unthinking states. In this book, I have discussed complex philosophical notions of who we are; what it means to be human; how we think and understand our world and what it is that each of us may be called to do with our lives. These are often thought of as rarefied discussions that are appropriate only at home or in a religion or philosophy class. But as Socrates famously said, an unexamined life is not worth living. So this book calls on each of us to examine our lives. It offers questions to help our reflections, but it is also clear to me that this task may seems onerous - largely unwanted, unsupported, thankless and certainly hard to master, especially in isolation. I understand the difficulty of engaging in deep reflection about the path the world is on and I also see how it can impact negatively on anyone who tries to take the time to reflect and think deeply.

It can seem a dangerous mission to focus on what has gone wrong in our world and to feel the resulting powerlessness to change anything. For me, climate change is the most daunting topic upon which to reflect. It seems we are quite literally rushing headlong as Max Weber said, into a 'polar night of icy darkness' (Chalcraft 2001). But John's writing gives hope that in encountering and reflecting on failure, weakness and uncertainty and in the freedom he finds in God's grace and within a community of love, we can become freed to see things differently and with imagination, hope and creativity. This freedom, along with the experience of solidarity with others, then gives us energy to act on the injustices we see in the world.

Political systems bring forth ways of organising ourselves in society that require us to abide by the rules of the society or be expelled or punished. This has been called the social contract. But a social contract should never require its members to stop being critical of situations that occur because of it. Yet in our times the social contract seems to require of us that we never question the way things are done and to accept what we are told as if it were Gospel.

As Mishra (2017:328) says

A managerial form of politics and neo-liberal economies have torn up the social contract. In the regime of privatization, commodification, deregulation and militarization it is barely possible to speak without inviting sarcasm about those qualities that distinguish humans from other predatory animals – trust, co-operation, community, dialogue and solidarity.

This is the very definition of ideology. As stated earlier in this book, ideology is a system of beliefs that is so pervasive as to be unquestioned. Yet it is, in fact, really just a set of beliefs. John argues that the ideology of modern times distorts reality in order to maintain the status quo and both renders invisible the harm that can be caused in our principal activity (work) and then necessarily marginalises the injured, sick or diseased (Bottomley 2015:27) to maintain the falsehood of hard work being its own reward.

The philosophers I have mentioned in this book– Hegel, Gramsci, Weber, along with the psychoanalytic thinkers – invite us to consider the pervasive nature of the capitalist system of beliefs, structures and practices that we are part of as an 'iron cage' and warn us that the future we are heading to is a 'polar night of icy darkness' (Weber 1905/1958:181 and Chalcraft 2001:216). This is ideology: we do not think daily that we are in an iron cage or heading to this apocalyptic polar night. Instead, we accept the prevailing ideology – we think this is just how things are.

Hegemony is where a dominant philosophy, social group or power elite controls others in that society. As said earlier, Gramsci argues that the hegemony of capitalism is cultural hegemony. In cultural hegemony, those with power carefully manipulate the social tools at their disposal to impose their ideology on the mass population to have them accept as perfectly normal those things that serve the ruling group. This is done (according to Gramsci) in church, school and in business. What is good for business is supposedly good for everyone and thus the foundation of the social order is not questioned.

A typical example of hegemony from the corporate sector is the franchising of businesses such as KFC, Starbucks, McDonalds all over the world, where not only the way of doing business is globalised, but so is the cuisine on offer. But a 2019 Australian parliamentary report on the franchise sector (Parliamentary Joint Committee on Corporations and Financial Services (2019) *Fairness in Franchising*) has uncovered a litany of horrific business practices based on a destructive business model that perpetrated price gouging, unconscionable contract arrangements, poor quality products, rampant under-payment of staff, tax fraud and bullying.

We are not discussing abstract concepts in this book that have no meaning in the 'real world'. These concepts have profound impact on people's lives. In the 1990s, the State Government Authority, Melbourne Water, lost some 6,000 employees over the decade, with a massive 31,% decline in one year alone.[40] During the time of these redundancies, three Melbourne Water staff took their own lives.

John Bottomley (1997) wrote a report on this sad fact called, *The Pressure is Enormous: the hidden costs of corporatisation*. The previously government-owned water board was privatised and corporatised purportedly in order to save money and reduce debt

---

40 Melbourne water Annual *Report* 1993-94, p. 2 as cited in Bottomley (1997).

for the Victorian State Government. But the changes were 'sold' as the best way of empowering workers to become self-fulfilled and to develop an entrepreneurial spirit. In a survey conducted with the Australian Services Union, the truth was that workers felt increased work pressure due to so many redundancies, greater responsibility, less capacity to supervise contracted work, but not necessarily greater freedom at work. And along with the greater responsibility came more stress, lower morale, poor job security, less time with family and increased family conflict.

The focus in the 1990s on corporatisation and, later, on corporate governance as the means to drive innovation, efficiency and economic growth may sound perfectly reasonable, but it is often built on a foundation of fear about scarcity. The focus is primarily on saving money or making more money, rather than on making a harmonious workplace that adds to the wellbeing of staff. How can any change at work that brings about the suicide of three workers be anything but unjust?

German philosopher, Theodor Adorno said people who operate as isolated consumers or individual competitors in capitalism are *completely cold who cannot endure their own coldness and yet cannot change it. Every person today, without exception, feels too little loved, because every person cannot love enough* (Adorno 1966:7). Klein's and Bion's theories suggest that from our earliest days, we see ourselves in relation to others and we define ourselves in relation to others and the experiences we have with them.

Evidence from many fields of science (neuroscience, biology and sociology) demonstrates that Hegel, Klein and Bion are right: we are formed only in relation to others. Modern day psychotherapist Sarah Sutton (2017:1) says it is, in fact, untenable now to *think of minds as an individual possession, each of us in the driving seat of our own little self-vehicle.* These new theories suggest that it is indeed cultural hegemony and not fact, to suggest that each of us is the individual master of his/her own destiny.

A good example of the inability to think outside the current system is embodied in the focus on governance that came about after the period of privatisation and corporatisation of public entities in the 1990s. In the decade of the 2000s, the church too became worried about scarcity and the risk of financial failure (after two Uniting Care aged care facilities incurred financial losses). It developed a *Governance Policies Manual and Workbook* based on a consulting firm's reports (Boardworks International) and using the Carver model of governance. It required its aged care and community service agencies to adopt the Carver model of governance. But this model is from the USA and advocates that all organisations can be subject to the rational and logical aims of the model. In fact, Carver claims 'universality' in the model. *It applies to governing boards of all types—non-profit, governmental, and business—and in all settings, for it is assembled from universal principles of governance.*[41]But in using this model, did the Uniting Church fall victim to hegemonic thinking? Are community service agencies corporate businesses?

There was limited theological critique or reflection at the time of its introduction and imposition on Uniting Church community service and aged care agencies. There was no opportunity to reflect that this model of doing business may not fit well with church agencies. Agencies were asked to create and adopt policies regarding results they wanted to achieve, governance of the agency, board-CEO relationship polices and limitations policies on the authority of the CEO. I know from conversations with John that he was reviewing the Book of Isaiah at this time, where a vision of God's governance is spelled out

---

41   J. Carver and M. Carver, 'Carver's Policy Governance Model in Nonprofit organizations', www.carvergovernance.com p.1

with God's rule decisively enacted and God's people are sustained in faithful worship. God's governance of the world is placed at the centre; it is first and foremost and without it, people in the Book of Isaiah fall into idolatry. God's governance calls for right relationship, justice, peace and care for one another. It must be put first.

With a concern for justice for the poor, God, in the Book of Isaiah, acts to free God's people from the folly of economic, political and social idolatry, and to uphold the urgent need for social inclusion. If there is a universal principle of governance, then surely it is not the Carver model, but instead it stems from this precept? Shouldn't Uniting Church institutions ask first: what is God's purpose for this organisation? Yet again, the Uniting Church seeks business solutions for the fear of risk and loss. As we have seen, even this did not appear to allow enough control over Uniting agencies and subsequently all aged care agencies were brought under the control of one board and then in 2016 most of the community service agencies were subsumed into one board with one set of rules to govern them. In his book with Howard Wallace, John says

While Carver/BI shape their governance theory around a story of fear and risk, with the Board and CEO acting as agents of control and security, agencies with an Isaianic imagination will be shaped by authentic worship that seeks to discern God's presence in the world. The stories of oppression, victimhood and liberation they encounter are interpreted within the cosmic, international and national stories of God's governance. These are stories the whole Church will need to hear in worship and discern a response. (Wallace & Bottomley 2012:184).

I don't want to give the impression that I am against any form of ethical governing of a not-for-profit agency. I am very clear that in the absence of structures, personalities will dominate and that organisations do need to be clear on where they are heading and what they hope to achieve. What concerns both John and me is the wholesale adoption of models from overseas, which do not allow for any local nuance and particularly the adoption of models developed to govern profit-generating businesses by charitable agencies, as if they are exactly the same type of enterprise. The prevailing ideology is invisible to us again – what works in the private sector is good and must be applied to the public and not-for-profit sector and workplaces are locations of rational, self-interested persons who engage in activities for the buying and selling of services and labour. All that is required are policies and procedures to ensure the key relationships of exchange are codified.

For John, the key failing of this view is that the church adopted the recommendations of a consulting firm and applied them to bodies, which are meant to be going about God's work on earth. He says the Carver model puts earthly rules ahead of God's law. And he is correct, because this is explicitly stated in the consultant's reports, where they note 'The board owes its paramount accountability'[42] to the legal owners, the UCA Synod. By adopting the Carver model of risk management and governance, agencies accepted the prevailing orthodoxy that there is no higher power than the state and the economy.

The reports, however, seek no information on compliance with, or faithfulness to, for example, God's justice. BI's governance theory constructs UC agency accountability as a closed system with ultimate

---

42 BI, *Governance Policy Guidelines*, p. 14.

allegiance to human structures. While agencies may proclaim they owe ultimate allegiance to God, Carver's governance theory and BI's policy advice for UCVT agencies ignores and diminishes this possibility. (Wallace & Bottomley 2008)

Often in his writing, John uses the term idolatry, meaning worshipping or placing reverence on something or someone who is not God. In the case of the Carver governance program, John argues that the knowledge of an expert is taken as fact. It is spoken of as if it is the universal, uncontested truth, and God is pushed to the margins. This is idolatry. John calls on the church to stop adopting business models arising from fear, risk and the scarcity of money and instead seek God's guidance in governing the work of the church.

> John asks the poignant question: what risk management strategy can ever hope to manage the risk posed by agencies shifting their allegiance from God's governance of their life and purpose to a human model that puts itself in the place of God as a universally accepted model?

This, too, is what the prophet Amos is trying to tell the people of Israel in the Old Testament: don't bother with your songs of praise if you are not out in the world making relationships right. In fact, Amos is scathing and says God 'hates' their festivals and disdains their assemblies, and the consequence of this turning away from God is that God's people will fall into exile, the reality of life cut off from its source in God's justice and mercy. The question may be whether this is the prospect facing Uniting and the Synod for their participation in their denial of God's governance? (Amos 8:9-10).

Psalm 135:15-18 expresses the worthlessness of gold and silver and the end result of idolatry (or commodity fetishism). In Marxist terms, commodity fetishism is a particular form of reification, where goods are imbued with the ability to bring happiness in and of themselves.

> *The idols of the nations are silver and gold, made by human hands.*
> *They have mouths, but cannot speak; eyes, but cannot see.*
> *They have ears, but cannot hear; nor is there breath in their mouths.*
> *Those who make them will be like them; and so will all who trust in them.*

Reification is a term not often used these days, but it means making an abstract concept — falsely and mistakenly — into a concrete thing. So a concept such as love may be reified these days by the showy display of an expensive wedding. The concept that is signified becomes only the material or concrete thing that we see and the true meaning of the concept is thereby lost. Similarly, money becomes a symbol for happiness, when clearly it does not necessarily bring happiness and, as a concept, happiness is much broader than that.

Reification is akin to what John calls idolatry. He talks often in his reports and books about putting false idols in place of God. Reification is the concept I use because it encompasses more than simply the dictionary definition of idolatry as the glorifying things and making them seem as if they have the power of gods. Reification is a dialectical transfer of understanding and mediation in a society, where members of the society come to understand the 'rules' of connection and action by exchange. John would certainly argue with me that while the dictionary defines idolatry as the worshipping and fetishism of idols, the consequences of doing so in a biblical sense are, in fact, dire in terms of God's judgment. He tells me that the notion of God's judgment is intrinsic to the prophetic literature about idolatry.

It seems to me that both idolatry and reification are complex terms to explain a similar notion; that we are not in relationship correctly at this point in time, essentially because we put high value on things, not on what God wants of us. The social contract (to use that term again) in capitalism allows for the value of things only to be deduced from the buying and selling of them. Things (and indeed people) have no intrinsic value in themselves, only what they are worth in a market. We do have a general tendency to make complex concepts more easily understood by having physical items stand in for them (calling climate and weather 'mother nature' for example) and this is understandable. But in a society based entirely on the buying and selling of goods and services for private ownership, there is no opportunity for connection and relationship except through the transaction of buying and selling. Each person is alone in the buying and selling of goods and services and each person gives meaning to this action, as though they were engaging in social relationships, but where really the only relationship is between the things being traded.

> *Since individuals do not enter into productive relations with one another directly as social beings, but only as owners of particular things, the possession of things becomes a condition for and determines the nature of each individual's participation in the productive relations of society.* (Burris 1988:6)

For Marx, commodity fetishism describes the 'mystery' we see in the transaction of goods as they stand in for higher order concepts. The buying and selling of everything begins to seem perfectly natural and the 'personification of things' comes to represent all there is in the social system. Marx tells us that capital (money or wealth) becomes seen as only available as privately owned, not socially owned. Similarly, the concept of private land ownership becomes seen as meaning simply 'land'.

The First Fleet and later British arrivals to Australian shores were also unable to see the concept of land in any other way: someone must own it, if they do then we can buy it, but if no-one owns it, then it is ready to be owned and ours to take. It was quite an alien concept to think of land as the sustaining earth that cannot be owned. In reification, we lose the ability to see the concepts behind the physical stand-ins we, as humans, create for them and we come to believe the stand ins to be the natural order. We believe this to be a *natural and intrinsic substantive character belonging to them, as it were, from time immemorial* (Marx, *Capital* as quoted in Burris 1998:9).

In John's view, such blindness to the human made way of interacting in our society must be challenged by the church so that a new and creative means of organising ourselves in society can come about. Undoubtedly those with wealth, power and authority in this current epoch are unlikely to offer to give up their position, so change needs to come from a body which is in the world, but not of the world, such as the church.

Do not be conformed to this world, but be transformed by the renewal of your mind, that by testing you may discern what is the will of God, what is good and acceptable and perfect (Romans 12:2)

The role of the church

As an outsider to regular worship in a church, I see a rather moribund organisation. It has an old fashioned way of engaging with matters of a spiritual nature. It seems to be largely made up of elderly people in grand buildings and it seems insular and individual. But this is just my perception. The facts are that church attendance is in decline and its relevance is questioned. Between 1993 and 2009, the proportion of Australians attending a service of worship monthly or more often dropped from 23 per cent to 16 per cent. Occasional attendance (less than monthly) also dropped from 42 per cent to 36 per cent.[43]

The focus of church-based worship does seem to be modelled on a bygone era with a fantasy of rural village life at its centre, and coming from a distant country. And it seems that this model of local, geographically-based congregations is the 'best and only model' the churches can conceive of or allow. John noticed in his early research that the institutional church did not support and indeed actively opposed its ministers from taking up positions outside of the sanctioned congregational placement model (Bottomley 2015:14). And it does need to be acknowledged that the various churches hold great tracts of land and buildings in which very little appears to be happening that changes the inequalities we see around us.

The primary focus of the traditional church is on the congregation meeting at the church on Sundays and the congregational focus on a traditional Christian church is the 'hearth and home.' The church has had little to say to people grieving injustice, outside the private world of home and family. Few congregations offer support to their members about their work if they are in paid employment.

While the work-related causes of injustice appear to pile up, today the church's voice for justice on these matters appears mute. It is as if these injustices are hidden from

---

43 https://cra.org.au/factors-in-declining-church-attendance/

the eyes of ministers, congregations, presbyteries and synods. (Wallace & Bottomley 2012:71)

With the rise of professional community services agencies, historically auspiced by the church, and the relegation of worship to the Sunday Service, another binary becomes apparent. The problem (for me) with this is the split created between secular, professional bodies that offer relief to those in poverty without a theological basis for critiquing the prevailing system that creates this poverty. The good work done by agencies is based on a professional model of psychology or social work, education or personal care. It is, therefore, not theologically underpinned. Looked at in this way, we can see that the church agencies have abandoned their call from God to fight injustice wherever they see it. In church worship, the focus is on the home and family and in professional agencies, the focus is on assisting the most marginalised. Where are the calls from the church to increase justice at work?

I have noted earlier that in our published article *Has God Stopped Calling?* (Dempsey & Bottomley 2011) John and I argue that the traditional congregation-based church is fearful that it is no longer relevant in the 21st century. But rather than search out, pray for God's guidance, open discussion and relationship, model and support new forms of church in order to be relevant, it hangs on tenaciously to its 19th century structure and models of worship. We also think that at a deeper level, the church fears that in facing and admitting its institutional decline, there is a dimly perceived sense of God's abandonment of the present form of church. The institutional church does not have to remain in the same structure and with the same focus it had in times gone by. But it seems the church has succumbed to the fantasy of its own inevitability (Levine 2005). It cannot imagine itself no longer present and it cannot envisage itself in any other form.

If the church believes itself to be wholly good and that it exists to show the way, then it may feel an imperative to ensure its survival in its present form. In all his writings, John calls on the Uniting Church to discern what God might be saying to it in the face of indisputable evidence of its institutional decline. But there seems little sign of any such discernment in the proclamations, statements and activities of the institutional Uniting Church.

I agree with John that if the church is to heed to the Word of God (which it seemingly stands for) then it ought to be at the forefront of calls for justice. The church needs to be in the world calling out injustice and working towards equality. This very issue is discussed in a recent statement by Pope Francis where he reminds the Catholic Church of its role:

I dream of a "missionary option", that is, a missionary impulse capable of transforming everything, so that the Church's customs, ways of doing things, times and schedules, language and structures can be suitably channelled for the evangelization of today's world rather than for her self-preservation. [44]

The Pope goes on to say he does not think the parish is an out-dated institution if it is capable of self-renewal and adaptation, but it has to ensure it does not become *a self-absorbed group made up of a chosen few*. But next he says other church institutions are a source of enrichment with *a new capacity for dialogue with the world whereby the Church is renewed*. I can find no similar statement from the Uniting Church that indicates both

44 http://w2.vatican.va/content/francesco/en/apost_exhortations/documents/ papa-francesco_esortazione-ap_20131124_evangelii-gaudium. html#I.%E2%80%82A_Church_which_goes_forth. Sections 27,28,29.

that it sees that it has a mission to fight evil in the world and that it understands that this may require discernment and change to its role, structure and focus for the sake of the world and not for its own self-preservation.

Most critical of all in John's writing is his belief that the churches are complicit in this acceptance of our current system of modernity as the best system we can have. On page 31 of *Hard Work Never Killed Anybody*, he says *[T]he church that I grew up in...is complicit in sustaining the ideology of work.* If we believe in the power of hard work to get us everything we need to live a whole and meaningful life, then we dismiss those for whom this has not worked out. The sick, the vulnerable, the stranger, the traumatised are not worthy of our support - rather we can separate ourselves from them and dismiss them as they simply brought their problems on themselves by not working hard enough.

John argues that the capture of the church in the prevailing heresies of modern (western) life can be seen right at the beginning with the *Basis of Union* document proclaiming the new Uniting Church in 1977 (in Australia) but which contained no reference to the bitter divisions that occurred at that time between the Protestant churches which did (or did not) join the Uniting Church.

From day one, the UCA has been captive to the modernist ideology that promotes forgetfulness of injustice in power relations; which lives at a distance from the reality of injustice, pain and grief....[a] church that can so comprehensively live in denial of the suffering and weakness experienced then, today finds itself trapped in an ideology of reconciliation that has little spiritual depth to respond... (Bottomley 2015:116)

John is particularly scathing when criticising his own church for its failure to comment publicly on working life, to call out and fight injustice at work and to support those who have suffered during their working lives.

Here is a church captive to the idol of hard work and the illusion that the church's salvation is in its own hands. By forgetting its own pain, the church has also forgotten it only lives in the Body of Christ, crucified and risen...the Uniting Church's captivity to the spirituality of modernity in its journey to union reveals the depth of this Australian church's theological crisis. This captivity is paralysing its ability to see and hear Christ's call to repent of its idolatry and turn in solidarity to those burdened by the depths of trauma and grief perpetrated by a society founded on injustice. (Bottomley 2015:117)

It is a very significant thing indeed for an ordained Minister of the Word in the Uniting Church to both stay in the church and yet be so openly critical of it. Think about it: John is essentially a representative of an organisation that he feels has utterly lost its way. But more damning than having lost its way, it perpetuates lies about how the world works, its own role and purpose and its essential 'goodness' as an organisation. This is strong critique indeed.

There are, of course, other views of the church and its work and it is an organisation of many individuals each trying to find a way in our complex world. But I find considerable merit in John's thesis that the church has been and remains part of the enterprise of empire. Many churches are built on crown land, which was "given" to them by the government (including St George's, where John was a minister). But this was land taken from local Aboriginal people. The church is caught in the myth of progress, which suggests that through overlooking and 'forgetting' injustice and moving forward relentlessly, rationality and hard work will secure a trouble-free and prosperous future - all those who work hard are rewarded.

When the Creative Ministries Network was subsumed into Uniting, the key reasons given were economic – the Agency needed better systems and governance; it required better fiscal oversight. In a rather typical capitalist view of money, its church appointed review body at the time saw the agency's plans to spend its financial resources (rather than make a profit or break even) as irresponsible. But as Chair of the Board of CMN at the time, I agreed with my board colleagues (past and present) that to spend our wealth in offering the best service possible to those most in need was the best way to be in the world. We determined to spend our resources until the money ran out and/ or until some further money was found. We felt the best way to combine Word and deed was to spend our funds in an abundant manner, with the hope that further funds would arrive because of the size and scope of the work we were doing.

For us, this seemed in keeping with the Gospel of abundance and hope. But the review body was trapped in the iron cage of rationality and unable to see any other way of doing God's work, but to save resources, invest them prudently and parcel them out in a miserly fashion so they could last as long as possible. A promise was made that CMN would 'flourish' inside the new structure of Uniting. Perhaps it is still early days, but I cannot see any growth of effort or energy for looking closely at the issues that John raised over his career. I do not see how our resources (now controlled by Uniting) have been used for the purposes the CMN originally intended. Is Uniting directing its energies to the world of work and to increasing justice at work? Is it questioning the cultural hegemony of our times? Is it seeking to know what God might be saying to it as it goes about seeking government funding for its programs?

The Uniting Church says so little publicly, in theological terms, of the likely wrath of God for the sins we all see around us. Indeed, the 'Protestant work ethic' is a ubiquitous phrase of derision these days – even in Weber's time it was considered devoid of any spiritual content and merely a support for the barons of capitalism to make profit on the backs of working people.

Here is what the Pope said in 1981 on justice in the workplace (and there is a long history of Catholic Popes commenting on justice at work):

We must "save working people from the cruelty of men of greed, who use human beings as mere instruments for money-making. It is neither just nor human so to grind men (and women) down with excessive labour as to stupefy their minds and wear out their bodies."[45]

In the National Church Life Survey of 2016 in Australia, 49% of regular churchgoers were employed. But inside the Protestant churches it is as if what goes on every day in the working life of a person for 40-50 hours a week is of no consequence. John said: -

I grieve that the certainties of my youth have crumbled and that the church I grew up in, by our retreat into the private world of home and family, is complicit in sustaining the ideology of work. But through this grief, God was taking a hand also in my formation for ministry. (Bottomley 2015:31)

---

45 http://w2.vatican.va/content/john-paul-ii/en/encyclicals/documents/hf_jp-ii_enc_14091981_laborem-exercens.html 1981

On so many occasions, the Bible is clear that the church has a role in exposing injustice wherever it may be found – including the workplace.

> *So I will come to put you on trial. I will be quick to testify against sorcerers, adulterers and perjurers, against those who defraud labourers of their wages, who oppress the widows and the fatherless, and deprive the foreigners among you of justice, but do not fear me," says the LORD Almighty.* (Malachi 3:5)
> *Look! The wages you failed to pay the workers who mowed your fields are crying out against you. The cries of the harvesters have reached the ears of the Lord Almighty.* (James 5:4)

In John's view, it is the role of the church to be a prophetic voice. It will do this when it stands in solidarity with those who bear the burden of injustice and oppression, when it speaks the truth of people's suffering to those in power, joins those who suffer in public lament before God of their experience of injustice and suffering, and empowers those captive to unjust powers to envision a new possibility for their lives gifted by God's healing, justice and reconciling power. It needs to speak the truth about the injustices occurring in the world today. In fact, John wrote an entire book (with Howard Wallace) called *Hope for Justice and Reconciliation* on the writings of the Old Testament prophet, Isaiah, relating his truth-telling and foretelling to the current social and political situation in Australia.

A prophet is someone who tells the truth about the existing conditions we find ourselves in and also tells of the likely fallout from our turning away from the true path. In the Old Testament, prophets were largely scorned for telling the truth to Israel about how it had turned away from God's path and they were not rewarded for foretelling God's punishment for doing so.

In their book, John and co-author Howard Wallace note that the churches' long involvement in social welfare programs demonstrates their prophetic stance, in that these programs and activities testify that things are not right and that some people are missing out or being left behind.

The very fact that these services were needed and provided gave voice to a prophetic critique that something was wrong with the status quo (Wallace & Bottomley 2012:55)

The fact that the need for these services continues and that more and more money is poured into government funding of social service programs and activities demonstrates that things are not improving. The system that allows or causes these injustices to happen is not changing for the better. Isaiah might say, we are not listening to what God wants of us. CEOs of UnitingCare social services (as quoted in Wallace & Bottomley 2012), comment that the increasing incorporation of their programs into a market economy is draining their agencies of life. They highlight issues such as having to compete for tendered projects, having to account for every cent spent, the focus on risk and the siphoning of resources into the complex regulatory environment of the business world, making creative and innovative responses to peoples' needs very difficult to establish or maintain. Given this context, a social service staff member may want to reflect on where is God's voice in their work? What does God call me to do?

The prophetic voice says that chaos and emptiness are the only responses possible for a sick society that does not heed the call of the prophet to turn back to God's will and purpose (Wallace & Bottomley 2012:64).

Word and Deed

In 1994 (a full twenty-five years ago), a report was commissioned by the Uniting Church in Victoria, arising from a 'widespread call from the Church's agencies and programs for a greater sense of common direction and purpose' (Linossier 1994). It followed an earlier attempt to outline the connection between the faith and community service agencies in 1986, which was never completed. In 2012, as a consultant, I undertook a similar review of agencies and their associated councils and congregations. I am not aware of any change occurring as a result of my work in 2012. No doubt there have been other reports too. Paul Linossier's 1994 report raises what it calls the 'twin challenges' of rediscovering the gospel in the midst of our work and rediscovering the place of mission in our faith communities.

So it is clear that the call to find a sense of connection between the church's worshipping congregations and the programs and actions of church agencies has had a long and lamentable history. The key issues in 1994 were listed as:

- the development of a theological basis for our work
- a closer examination of our relationship with
  government
- the development of a strong social justice approach,
  including policy analysis and advocacy
- the enabling of congregations and parishes to
  rediscover mission.

It seems to me that in 2019 these connections are still needed but we are no closer to achieving them. Why after so long, are they still not happening? In many church documents, I read the importance of 'word and deed'. In the *Basis of Union*, the church is called upon to 'confess to the Lord in fresh words and deeds'. In community service agencies reports and plans, I read about the importance of 'word and deed'.

If Uniting is to be a community service arm of the Uniting Church, then it needs to first acknowledge the Word. The Word of God is the preeminent word. It is the starting point, surely. But the meaning in these documents seems to be something more like speaking the truth, being ethical, matching our actions with our words and so forth. It seems as if there has (somehow) been a 'watering down' of the original meaning of the Word.

I know John is called an 'ordained Minister of the Word'. It is his task to tell the Word of God. I am reminded again here of the Hegelian dialectic and the possibility of creating something new from a contemplation of the meaning of the term 'Word and deed', rather than the rather pedestrian ways that we speak of 'word and deed', that frames our community services activities – yes, we want to be people of integrity in both what we say and do. But can we focus on the Word of God (however we may each frame it) and consider what that Word calls for us to do in this imperfect world?

The Word (as I understand it from a lay and agnostic perspective) is that God made the world and all the beautiful things in it and that we humans unfortunately turn away from how God wants us to care for this creation and live in peace. For things to 'go right' and be in balance or harmony, if you will, then we must first understand and acknowledge that this is the truth, and seek forgiveness for having messed things up. It seems to me to be self-evident that we have failed abysmally. In the religious sense, to have messed things up means to be out of favour with God or out of right relationship with God and therefore with what is the best we can each and collectively be. Is there something worth pondering in reflection about the part we each play in making ourselves the embodiment of the Word?

I put the quote from the Old Testament prophet Amos at the beginning of this book. In those verses, God is saying to Israel (when Israel is only paying lip service to worship) that God despises this because their worship is a sham. Their prayers and praise do not address the God of freedom and justice, but their own self-satisfaction. Rather, God seeks from them action that brings about justice and righteousness for all.

When we engage in government funded programs, we serve the agenda of the government; if we offer support to the disenfranchised with no sense of, or commitment to the change needed to embrace them, we serve the status quo; when we act in the name of the Uniting Church without acknowledgment of the history of abuse and neglect,[46] we ignore our capture to the prevailing power structures; if we act from a sense of superiority to those we help, we ignore their cry for justice and we unthinkingly serve and foster the existing unequal power relationships of our capitalist society.

In *Hope for Justice and Reconciliation*, John and Howard note their research of CEOs of UnitingCare Community Service Agencies (before they were subsumed into Uniting) that the worship that may occur in Sunday Services is largely disconnected from the work these CEOs do on behalf of the church. Their practice is rooted in their professional backgrounds, in evidence and outcomes, in seeking funding, in adopting a business model for funding community services and in avoiding censure from government for any advocacy efforts that may limit access to funding (Wallace & Bottomley 2012:46).

The community services agencies of Uniting are essentially secular: accountable to secular and government accountability

---

46 see case study 56 of the Royal Commission Into Institutional Responses to Child Sex Abuse.https://childabuseroyalcommission.gov.au/sites/default/files/case_study_56_-_opening_address_-_institutional_review_of_uniting_church_in_australia_-_sydney.pdf

regimes. Decisions by Synod (not necessarily with this intent) have led to yet another example of a binary, having split worship from mission. The separation of the corporate life of UnitingCare agencies from their life of faith was created by the Synod (Bottomley 2015:83). But this separation of corporate and faith life is not the way that the CMN and its predecessor agencies operated. They made efforts to integrate Word and deed, faith and mission. They made a commitment to being a prophetic ministry, with all actions flowing from a faith in God who loves those whom this society casts aside (Bottomley 2015:85). A prophet is the privileged and burdened recipient of divine revelation given for the realisation of God's will on the earth. The prophetic voice stands in opposition to the powers that be and calls for change. The prophet hears the voice of those unjustly treated and stands in solidarity with them.

John has told me on many occasions of the struggle and inspiration of trying to live faith and mission. In *Hard Work Never Killed Anybody*, he writes that the CMN Board's commitment to speaking the language of faith created a workplace that accepted various expressions of spirituality and brought to light a diverse range of insights into faith. It led to a creative and expansive openness to trying new ways of doing and being (Bottomley 2015:86). But does Uniting encourage and support this way of being church?

The *Basis of Union* document that formed the Uniting Church (from Methodist, Congregationalist and Presbyterian churches) makes no mention of the struggle to get to union and of the Protestant denomination which did not join it. For John, this is an example of not heeding the voices of those disenfranchised. The first step on the path of joining Word and deed is to acknowledge this situation, confess the truth of this situation (sin perhaps?), openly lament the suffering that accompanied it, as in the process of restorative justice (outlined earlier) and with grace, recover hope for healing. Without this process, the emptiness, chaos and the clutching at straws will continue to be felt and acted upon, as God's judgment (Wallace & Bottomley 2012:69).

Questions for Reflection on this Chapter

This chapter covered major themes that run through the work of John Bottomley. It calls on the reader to take time to reflect on these themes and see whether anything resonates with you when you ponder them. It invites you to read more about the ideas to gain a better understanding of them.

- Which part of the chapter is most revealing to you? What did you find yourself resisting? Why?
- When have you spoken truth to others, especially those with power?
- What made that possible? What prevents you from speaking in the ways you may desire?
- Is this 'call to mission' for churches from the Pope something you can relate to? What might it mean for you?
- What do you feel about the need for adaptation in either your personal sense of mission or in your work environment and why?
- Do you find John's view compelling, or do you find yourself arguing with his point of view?
- A prophetic view seeks to speak truth to power. Does this happen today in Australia? Do you know of any person or group that is taking up that challenge? Do you have a role to play?
- What does the church need to do to transform itself (if you agree it does need to transform)?
- Have you ever worked with a 'prophet' (someone who sees things very differently to everyone else)?
- How easy or hard was it to be open to hearing their views?

CHAPTER 5

FINDING THE LIMINAL SPACE

You need to know what it means to be restored in your humanity so that you know restorative justice is at its core about the gift of love and the fruit of relationships. (Bottomley 2015:173)

Following the summary and interpretation of the key themes of John Bottomley's work, I now turn to what we can each do to increase justice in the world. We don't have to organise protest marches, chain ourselves to the houses of parliament (unless we feel compelled), but there are small things to do that can help change things for the better. In this chapter, I suggest that we start by a careful contemplation of what we each can do, whether we are comfortable with being 'prophets' calling out injustice and how to think together and alone about the contents of this book and of the thirty years of work of all those associated with the Urban Ministry Network, the Centre for Creative Ministries and the Creative Ministries Network.

I think it is time for reflection! Reflection helps to slow down decision-making and allows more complexity to be tolerated in the way we look at events and issues. Reflection is helpful to see the part we each play in a given situation, instead of blaming others or outside events for unexpected results or for problems and difficulties. It is the beginning to finding that elusive liminal space that I have used in the title of this chapter.

Practising Negative Capability

In 1817, the poet John Keats wrote to his brother about the essential characteristics of great writers and poets. He named this quality negative capability. He didn't mean negative in a pejorative sense, but rather he was referring to the capability to sit quietly and not 'do' anything, to be in doubt, wonder and reflection, rather than be busy in the world of action. Keats words[47] were: -

I mean Negative Capability, that is when a man is capable of being in uncertainties, Mysteries, doubts, without any irritable reaching after fact and reason

Threaded throughout John Bottomley's work is a call for the reader to reflect on what it means to be human. In his work, John asks us, his readers, to practise negative capability. Although he does not use the term coined by Keats, he asks us, first, to sit quietly and reflect, to marvel at the power of story to inspire, to wonder at the earth and the joyous creation around us: to consider life and the earth as gifts to be treasured and supported. This sort of reflection gives opportunity to hear the 'voice' of emotion and imagination, as well as that of reason and the intellect.

Quiet reflection helps us to see the good in all things – in all peoples and cultures, in all types of stories and experiences. It helps us to see the complexity and nuance of issues that arise before us. It helps us move from the model of scarcity and putting a price on things that is inherent in our modern lives, to the idea of the abundance of the earth to provide for our needs. It slows us down from reaching for fact, reason and solution. It certainly does not blind us to the evils that exist in the world, but it gives us a freedom to imagine a better world and to offer action to

47 http://www.keatsian.co.uk/negative-capability.php

bring this about. It then calls us to name the evil around us. But quiet reflection requires practice and a maturity to attain.

What is liminal space?

I have written elsewhere about the concept of the liminal space.[48] The concept came first from anthropology where it described the supplicant entering a ritual. In the ritual, the supplicant moves from their usual self to a place and space of confusion, ambiguity, unknowingness. This is the liminal space; the threshold, the border between two worlds; the edge or frontier. After some time here, the supplicant emerges from the ritual transformed. Liminal space is the transition place where we move from what we know and who we are to something new and as yet unformed. In a sense, it is the space between binaries.

Our busy working lives offer little respite from action, worry and rushing; and little or no support for entering this liminal space and holding the space for quiet contemplation. But it seems to me that this is the place to start if we are hoping to make the world a better place. Without this reflection, the extremes of the world of action will pull and push us – we either manically rush around trying to solve problems and control or fix everything or we become stuck; we can quickly feel overwhelmed by the hopelessness of the situations we encounter and unable to see the possibility of doing anything useful.

Finding a Balance

Both these positions are unhelpful because they are binary (again). We either feel omnipotence in what we can and must achieve, leading us to believe we have the answers to solve

---

48 *Desire and Accommodation: Finding a Liminal Space.* Presentation to the regional meeting of the International Society for the Psychoanalytic Study of Organisations. Melbourne 2017 (unpublished, available from author)

problems for clients and customers, without for a moment walking in their shoes or asking what they might actually want and need – or indeed contemplating how a supposedly fair and egalitarian society allows their suffering to occur. As a consultant, all too often I have seen this attitude in community service workers. It is as if getting too close to a needy client may 'infect' us somehow and slow us down from finding solutions. So we detach ourselves from the pain and suffering that we see by working harder to get a client off the books; the client referred to a relevant service; housing found or government support arranged. All of these activities are laudable, but they diminish the personhood of the client if they occur without deep consultation about what is required and desired by the whole person – body and spirit.

Alternatively, community services workers can feel simply overwhelmed by the task. This is commonly referred to as 'burn out' or 'compassion fatigue'. In this case, they see the same problems over and over again and feel that nothing ever changes. So, they might do the bare minimum to manage their daily tasks and again avoid close contact with clients to avoid entering the liminal space with them, not truly hearing their story and attending to the needs of the whole person. There could be a real fear in any work with vulnerable or marginalised members of society that coming too close may damage the worker too. It may be overwhelming and paralysing to see, hear and attend to the true suffering in front of us.

I am well aware, too, of the pressure to measure and quantify all that we do at work. Funding bodies require an account of how well their money is being spent and so they require complex metrics to be employed to tally up our productivity. But often relationship is lost in the focus on key performance indicators.

When a service is busy counting how many phone calls it receives, how many clients it sees, how many reportable incidents occur, Workcover claims made, complaints made, checks completed, referrals made, cases closed, training undertaken, audits passed and the like, then it is possible to become mired in the culture of audit and risk and lose sight of the true reason for the service. Trust in each other and in the desire to good work is supplanted by trust only in that which can be measured and counted as if only those are real and worthwhile.

In my view, our obsession with measuring and accounting for every action is a protective mechanism against the horrible truth that, just perhaps, we are not making any difference at all and that we do not have the mastery over our circumstances that we crave. It is a response to the importing of business models and ways of thinking into social services, where they do not belong. There is a sort of 'collective madness' in trying to quantify how well programs help those who do not fit society's expectations, so that they may better fit society's expectations. By doing so, we can avoid thinking deeply about the social expectations themselves and avoid considering if drug addiction, homelessness, poor health, work injury are understandable responses to abuse, neglect and violence. If we were to focus on the presenting issues of clients as legitimate responses, rather than problems to be dealt with, then surely we would need to consider that our society must change fundamentally. I know John sees these responses as manifestations of God's judgment.

Finding a way to stay with the complexity of the work and not 'retreat to' simplistic binary notions is the difficult path of the community service worker. The dilemma is how to help people every day and at the same time avoid being overwhelmed by the size of the problem or alternatively, judging the client for their failure to conform. Being able to take time to 'step outside' the role for a moment and reflect on this 'collective madness' as I call it could be a key to finding the liminal space.

I think it is a form of collective madness that we do not question the way our society works, but instead we help as best we can, whilst unquestioningly assuming that everyone is free, independent and has the benefit of equal rights. Deep reflection will help us to avoid a split (right vs. wrong) and over-simplistic position that sees clients as draining workers dry and that their need is never ending with scarce resources to deal with the issues. Or the alternative split position that clients are unco-operative and oppositional and never improve not matter what is done to help them. Instead reflection allows the 'to and fro' of ideas and to consider more complex connections to be made around the client's situation, the part we play as helping professionals and the economic system under which we all work.

But to achieve a mature and nuanced position in isolation would be extremely difficult, I imagine. Hearing stories helps to engender empathy and to see possibilities. We see our shared values and shared humanity as we listen. There can be many ways to evoke the heart-felt stories of others and to 'walk in their shoes'. There are things that can be done on the day-to-day and individual level as well as at the level of the system that we are part of and again at the cultural or societal level, to make change.

I offer a reflective cycle for individuals in Uniting to use to begin to see the world in which they live a little differently. My hope is that this type of reflection can help policy makers and workers see that they are part of a vast movement towards a better, more just future (rather than merely helping at the margins). I also call on Uniting to offer opportunities to change the system of applying for and winning grants and tenders by telling the stories of those they work with and advocating for them and with them to make sustainable change and I call on the church in Australia to be a prophetic voice that calls on society to change.

Let's think of John's work as a catalyst for systemic change; let's work for a safer and fairer society and walk alongside those who suffer injustice in our post-capitalist world. Let's call out the injustice that their individual situation demonstrates. Rather than focusing on offering professional help for those who suffer injustice, let's learn from their stories and walk alongside them as we navigate our way through an unfair system.

Working with the evil of the system as the starting point is key (as well as thinking of how to alleviate the suffering of the individual client). There was at least one occasion when funding (available from a particular government authority) came to CMN with so many conditions that were anathema to the CMN's approach that the organisation declined to apply - at considerable risk to its financial viability. It is possible to change the system by taking this type of risk. Today's current highly competitive funding environment puts pressure on agencies to win tenders – but sometimes at considerable risk to their ethics around staff terms and conditions, how services should really be delivered, and the impetus to keep silent about wider systemic deficiencies.

Companioning

John's later work focused on creative programs for clients, which he described as 'companioning' and 'peer support'. Peer support is a system of giving and receiving help founded on key principles of respect, shared responsibility and mutual agreement about what is helpful or not. The need for a peer support function in the workers compensation system was identified by participants in a research report by CMN into the experience of fifteen long-term injured workers (Pollock et al 2014).

Asked what could be done to address their needs, the injured workers stressed the importance of access to timely and comprehensive information, and having support (someone on their side) during the process to ensure that fairness and agency could be achieved within the system (Glass 2016). The CMN study found that the information and support that was most helpful came from a trusted source, such as a family member, medical professional, their union, and other injured workers. As one injured worker said, 'I would be helped if I had a buddy who had been through it who could be by my side'. Trust is established with the injured worker by the peer support worker through their shared experience of work injury.

Alan Wolflet[49, 50] is a North American grief counsellor who developed a companioning model of accompanying people who are dying, preferring to use the term companion instead of a rather professional term of 'treating' those who mourn. Here are his eleven principles: -

- Companioning is about being present to another person's pain; it is not about taking away the pain.
- Companioning is about going to the wilderness of the soul with another human being; it is not about thinking you are responsible for finding the way out.
- Companioning is about honouring the spirit; it is not about focusing on the intellect.
- Companioning is about listening with the heart; it is not about analysing with the head.

49 https://www.centerforloss.com/about-the-center-for-loss/about-dr-alan-wolfelt/
50 http://www.txnmhospice.org/docs/2017Conference/KeynoteHandouts-Feb24.pdf

- Companioning is about bearing witness to the struggles of others; it is not about judging or directing these struggles.
- Companioning is about walking alongside; it is not about leading or being led.
- Companioning means discovering the gifts of sacred silence; it does not mean filling up every moment with words.
- Companioning the bereaved is about being still; it is not about frantic movement forward.
- Companioning is about respecting disorder and confusion; it is not about imposing order and logic.
- Companioning is about learning from others; it is not about teaching them.
- Companioning is about curiosity; it is not about expertise.

You can see that Wolflet sees companioning as walking alongside the bereaved (in this instance) and listening in silence. It sounds very like the idea of negative capability described earlier. As we learned from the companioning model used by CMN and described in chapter three, when the bereaved are given unconditional and open-ended support, they rarely abuse that gift and 'over-use' the service. They want to move forward and regain some measure of governance over their own lives and when they have the back up support that is 'there if they need it', they only sometimes call upon it. The worry of over-dependence on service support comes more from the providers or funders of the service who fear that the support required might be a never ending abyss, rather than the reality of support that is actually requested. If the attitude of abundance can be maintained, then the fear of scarcity is minimised.

Companioning can provide opportunities to be with bereaved people and others who are suffering, on their own terms, together, in liminal space. There are ways to learn to stay in the moment of inaction, the moment of transformation and to be there is strangely energising, rather than energy draining. If we can hold this space, it allows the other to expand into the space and tell their story. We can try to listen in the moment and accept the story without judgment or rushing to find a solution. Try to focus on the other person and keep your own story out of the discussion, allow them to come to their own conclusion and decision, even if it is not would you would advise.[51]

John seems to have had an iterative, repetitive and reflective way of working – much as I am describing in this chapter. He would listen and notice what is really happening, hear from those who are being harmed, learn, discuss, study and reflect and then develop a theological perspective. John works in just the same way as the psychoanalysts and philosophers I have mentioned who speak of the importance of dialogue, relationship and of staying in uncertainty. Of course, John is deeply immersed in his faith, but his faith didn't take him down narrow pathways but seemed to open him up to new ways of thinking, new ways of framing issues and agency in the world. "The Word" seemed to open his imagination and creativity. His reflective practice together with his regular sessions of contemplative worship are evidence of this approach.

To stay in the place of careful listening, paying close attention to needs, desiring to help and acknowledging that sometimes our help is not working or not enough, is complex and mature work. It requires each of us to see the possibilities for hope and at the same time, it cultivates critical awareness of both personal and social evil. Yet like Hegel, we find in the

---

51 https://heatherplett.com/2015/03/hold-space/

dialectic that something new can be formed. But it is hard to achieve and maintain this dialectic alone. The prevailing culture does not support it.

Part of the purpose of this book, is to help community service workers to achieve solidarity, practise contemplation and reflection and share experiences with it. I believe John's hope was always that the Uniting Church would step up and offer support and solidarity with community service workers to achieve societal change. John would call this work the connection of Word and deed. By putting God at the centre of the work, we come to see that the way things are is not how they *must* be. We can walk alongside those for whom injustice is a fact of life, listen to their stories and their experience and call out injustice when we see it. In John's worldview, it means asking God what is required of him at a given time and waiting quietly for an answer to come.

Religious believers use the terms 'contemplation', 'discernment' and 'grace' in examining this experience. Contemplation is the quiet, still, reflective space where we allow ourselves to be open to whatever thoughts and feelings might come to us, and discernment is then judging whether a thought or feeling is merely our own ego or desire or perhaps comes from a deeper well of love for humanity and the earth. And grace, which is a lovely term in religious traditions means that despite our faults we are all deserving of love and so, with God's grace, we can see the way forward and be confident that we can make good decisions. If each of us can see the work of grace in our own lives, we can then see it in others.

But it takes reflective practice, slowing down and waiting, listening carefully for what is asked of you in every encounter with others. It means putting trust at the heart of every encounter so that relationships may flourish, not simply transactions of a reified nature. Keats called this negative capability, Wolflet called it companioning (when working with bereaved people) and the Daly River People call it dadirri. Being caught in the game of winners and losers, focusing on winning funding for government programs rather than questioning the way funding is provided (usually by tender and often to the lowest bidder) is not the way.

Dadirri

In the introduction to this book, I mentioned the term dadirri, from the Daly River People of the Northern Territory. In her explanation of the term for English speakers, Miriam Rose Ungunmerr-Baumann has said: -

Dadirri recognises the deep spring that is inside us. We call on it and it calls to us. This is the gift that Australia is thirsting for. It is something like what you call "contemplation".... It is inner, deep listening and quiet, still awareness... [t]here is no need to reflect too much and to do a lot of thinking. It is just being aware.

When I experience dadirri, I am made whole again. I can sit on the riverbank or walk through the trees; even if someone close to me has passed away, I can find my peace in this silent awareness. There is no need of words. A big part of dadirri is listening...

The contemplative way of dadirri spreads over our whole life. It renews us and brings us peace. It makes us feel whole again... In our Aboriginal way, we learnt to listen from our earliest days. We could not live good and useful lives unless we listened. This was the normal way for us to learn - not by asking questions. We learnt by watching and listening, waiting and then acting...

It became clear to me as I read and re-read John's work for this book, that he first tried to help others by examining their issues, and advising authorities on what needed to be done. But, later, he tried to listen more to people's stories of pain and emptiness and he looked for creative ways for people to express their stories and worked with them to find expression that resonated with them.

Narrative storytelling has a powerful integrative nature. It helps us make sense of our own lives and journeys. Richard Sennett (as noted earlier) argues that we are driven to create life narratives for ourselves in which work plays a big part in our sense of ourselves. The focus on rapid change, short-term jobs and episodes of work make life-long narratives and long-term values difficult to maintain. The nature of modern workplaces and practices undermines the values of trust, loyalty, commitment, and obligation to others. Increasingly, this change, in spite of greater freedom and the unprecedented development opportunities it purports to bring, can lead to feelings of insecurity and disorientation, which are experienced as loss.

John then focused on leaning in and listening to the stories he heard and waiting in quiet contemplation with people who came for help as they grappled with telling their story. It is the very nature of truly hearing individual stories that allows the discerning listener to see a pattern. Solidarity with others opens the spirit to the faults in our social system which blames victims for their own plight, sees individuals as failures, and ignores the voices of those who call out its injustices.

John's body of work is a call to action for both government and church bodies to do more, to do better, to build a more inclusive society. He argues that Christ's gospel calls workers in agencies like Uniting to be 'in the world' in solidarity with all those who struggle for a flourishing life in a precarious or fragile work environment. This means to do more than 'patch up' wounds encountered, but rather to advocate for change and to walk alongside those damaged by our dehumanising modernity and its systems (and that is all of us to some degree) and call for change.

But we can't stand up to the ideology of rationality alone. Solidarity is paramount to naming the lie that hard work never killed anybody, so the church has to step up. It has to be the alternative voice, the prophetic voice. And it is possible to make change. The 2016 National Church Life Survey found that 8/10 Australian church attenders would support the development of new initiatives in ministry and mission in their local church. This very high level of personal support of innovation is one of the hopeful findings from the 2016 National Church Life Survey. This increasing trend is among one of the most dramatic across 25 years of surveys.[52] Let's put it into action; let's make new congregations and new ways of being church, one that hears the pain of others and critiques the society in which it is situated.

The Reflection Cycle

This book takes the reflective cycle used in the Ignatian tradition as its starting point for thinking more deeply about the injustices of the system of capitalism. St Ignatius of Loyola was a Spanish Basque priest who wrote in the 16th century. Uniquely for the time, he strove for deep religious contemplation, which then allowed him (propelled him) to take action in the world. The religious order he established (the Society of Jesus or the Jesuits) was dedicated to work in the world and they moved to wherever they felt the need was greatest.

The concept of quiet reflection, leading to discerning the best action to take to improve your immediate situation is

---

52 http://www.ncls.org.au/news/2016-church-vitality-infographics

Reflection

Take the time to reflect on how your day went or on the issue at hand? What went well? What might help you to do better? What brings out the best in you? Look at what has been achieved already

Do More

Focus on peace, plenty and gratitude, rather than fear and anxiety. Think of what can be better tomorrow. Reflect again...

Discernment

Judge wisely. Be honest. What patterns can you see? What might help you to do better? What could you do differently? What was happening when you felt challenged or frustrated? What is the spirit behind your plans and activities - look for the good in them. Grant yourself mercy for not being perfect and then you can do so for others.

Action/Service

What do you want to achieve? What change can you make? What does the first step look like? It's OK to try and then try again

Focus on the whole person

Stay healthy, calm and rested. Find the better 'you' and care for yourself first, then care for others. Take the time to consider the unique gifts, talents and insights of yourself and others. Begin to think how to converge ideas and feelings from your reflection

Solidarity with others

Affirm the goodness of people and work with them. Respect the efforts of others. What concrete things can you do to improve things?

commonplace now in education with Gibbs' model being well known; and in psychology with Kolb's learning model prominent. It is also widely used in the health sector and readers can see more examples of reflective cycles online.[53]

They all have common features of taking the time to sit quietly and reflect on what happened and how you felt about it. They suggest you sit with both the good and bad feelings about the situation or event before you try to make sense of it. Allowing the feelings to come to the surface means that you do not rush, as Keats reminds us, after fact and reason. Instead, you allow yourself to feel. Then you consider what part you played in events and if anything could have been done differently. A consideration of the consequences for yourself and others is usually important. Finally, this type of reflecting leads to a consideration of what needs to be done about the incident or event being reflected upon, so that a better outcome occurs next time. To find new meaning and new ways of learning or interacting, the reflective practitioner must be able to sit in situations of uncertainty and ambiguity. It is in this phase (the liminal space) that new associations are made, new possibilities emerge and new ideas are formed.

The practice of reflection helps to shift the mind frame over time from believing that everything must be done in a rush, or that there is not enough time for the 'luxury' of sitting quietly. Connections are made between knowing and doing that lead to a more positive sense of possibility. Ideas come from this reflection and energy is released to enable the practitioner to try new things, see the world as a gift, be grateful for opportunities and look for the positives. Abundance, rather than scarcity, is seen as the true situation. For Ignatius, this is the starting point: that we see hope and the positive in all things we encounter.

---

53   https://latrobe.libguides.com/reflectivepractice/models

Your first thought may be that taking time out from a busy day for personal reflection is 'self-indulgent' and will lead to no improvement. It is surprising how often it does help in my experience and I know John has been practising this for over twenty years. Forms of reflection are a means, not an end. They are strategies in accomplishing the transformation of our world and ourselves. From my own experience and those of my colleagues, I would summarise the benefits like this:

- Pursuit of excellence[54]
- Respect for the world, its history and mystery
- Learning from experience
- Contemplative vision formed by hope
- Development of personal potential
- Critical thinking and effective communication
- Appreciation of things both great and small
- Commitment to service
- Special concern for the poor and oppressed
- Linking faith with justice
- International and global perspective
- Discerning mindset: finding God in all things.

St Ignatius used the term *cura personalis* which means care for the whole person. Part of reflecting is both caring for oneself and also for others that we work with. It means to discern how we can support ourselves to avoid our own burnout, and also work effectively with diverse groups for the common good. It is very much a term meaning *personal* care and, to my way of thinking, quite different from institutional care. It is about being closely involved and walking alongside others, paying special attention to the unique circumstances and concerns of the other,

---

54 http://www.loyno.edu/jump/about/loyola-at-a-glance/jesuit-tradition.php

with appreciation for their special gifts and talents. Reflective practitioners are able to take responsible action on moral and ethical issues and will thus be more prepared to be change agents in society.

In a similar way, Wilfred Bion tells us that learning occurs at the edges between knowing and not knowing (Simpson & French 2002). He urges psychoanalysts to stay in the space of 'alive waiting' with patience to wait for knowledge and understanding to come.

Discard your memory; discard the future tense of your desire; forget them both, both what you knew and what you want, to leave space for a new idea. (Bion 1980:11)

As a consultant, I find this experience occurs often. I am asked to come in to 'fix' a dysfunctional team or to train middle level managers to be better leaders. Let me describe how reflective practice informs my work. I begin by speaking to the people who seem to be 'causing' the problem. What I find invariably is that the situation is far more complex than is first described to me. I hear sadness and frustration. I hear blame and guilt. I start to internalise the fear I am hearing (who is to blame, what does the boss want, will I lose my job, what will this consultant do). I am brought to the edge of my knowledge: I don't know how to fix the problem when things seem so conjoined and messy. I feel the pressure of being the expert who is expected to find the answer – as if there is only one answer to be found. I realise I am at the edge of my capability and I feel anxious and worried about my own expertise to solve the problem.

When I feel these emotions and pay attention to them, I know that I am at the edge and need to wait for inspiration to come. I see that I am mirroring the feelings I have heard from the team. While it may not appear logical or rational, I begin to feel the same unwanted feelings that the team feels. Often I am told that "Cheryl is the problem" and we simply need to "get rid of her". I may start to believe this too. I get caught in the projection of all badness onto Cheryl, until I take the time to reflect and consider that it is too easy a solution to fire Cheryl. She may be acting badly for many reasons; she may have been drawn into this role of the "bad one" by pressure from others. I begin to see the split and binary nature of the workplace's desire to rid itself of badness by seeing it wrapped entirely in one person. I see my own desire to fix the problem, to look competent, and come in with the answer.

When this feeling comes upon me with its anxiety and its desire to rush to a solution, I recognise it well as I have been doing this type of consultancy and of reflection for many years. When I start to feel anxious and tempted to rush to a solution, then I know it is time to step back and wait. I am then able to offer my own confusion as a source of material for (confidential) talks with members of the team. This gives them the space for new ideas to come to the surface and the true work to improve the leadership or competence of a team can begin.

We see that we each act on and shape an event or incident by our own response to it: we are part of everything that goes on and the relationship is iterative, repetitive. In other words, the outcome is shaped by our repeated engagement with the elements of the situation. We are not separate, detached, objective observers (as the Enlightenment thinkers might have wanted), no, we are each part of the situation we are in. This is the form of research that Judy Atkinson (noted earlier) wants to see, where dadirri is practised in the way we interact and co-create a new story of hope and trust. We are not each called to "overthrow capitalism" singlehandedly and heroically, but we are each offered an opportunity, mostly noticed at times of crisis in our lives, to consider whether things could be better. Feeling positive and hopeful for the earth and its peoples is possible.

It is helpful if we can see options and consider if we can make more positive responses and help these options to develop. It is possible to change the way we live today. A good example is B Lab, which is a not-for-profit organisation based in USA, which created an idea to support and certify businesses that have a beneficial focus, whilst at the same time making profit on their activities.

B Lab started in 2006 and in the following thirteen years, it has grown as a movement all over the world. It certifies businesses in fifty countries that have 'benefit' as their key focus. They are called B-Corps and there are around 2,500 of them around the world.[55] The B Corp movement is positive and expansive in its attempts to drive social change by re-thinking how capitalism has been and how it could be in the future. The success of B Corp is the certification model. In other words, B Lab doesn't merely highlight "good" businesses; it goes about certifying them in a specific and concrete way. It, therefore, demonstrates that such businesses are possible, they can and do exist even as they put social and environmental sustainability at the core of their functioning. They agree to comply with higher standards of accountability and transparency in their operations.

It can be done. And it is happening in other spheres of organisational activity too. When I first commenced my working life, co-operatives existed where profit was distributed to the workers of the company and where they collectively made decisions about the business. In the intervening period, co-operatives seem to have gone out of favour in our race to the bottom with free market capitalism, based as it is on

55 https://bcorporation.com.au/

deregulation, globalisation and the political power of huge multinational companies. But I have noticed that co-operatives have a strong flourishing at the moment, perhaps in contrast to the enormous power wielded by multinational conglomerates. There are 30,000 cooperatives in the USA today.

What if we stopped saying "what if" and instead chose cooperatives as the business model of choice in your community and around the world? What if, through cooperatives, we chose to create a better world?[56]

The way the church is organised nowadays is for mission (actions in the world) to be split from worship. The typical geographic parish model of church excludes the public and political dimension of life. It ignores the workplace; it does not engage the structures of our society that are unjust. Concurrently, the community service model of mission accepts the status quo, not wanting to be outside and critiquing the system, but instead laying low, accepting government grants and their bureaucratic restrictions and receiving bequests or philanthropic funds to support victims. But in this model of parish worship and community service mission, we still see those who are assisted as victims and there is no mobilisation from the church to change the larger system. Instead, let's look at ways to change the system. There are good things going on to do just that. Examples of work for system change and cultural change are noted below:

Global Generation [UK][57]
We use land-based activities and the metaphors of ecological and cosmic processes to support building community between each other and the natural world. We primarily work with local young people,

---

56 https://cooperativesforabetterworld.coop/
57 https://globalgeneration.org.uk/about-us/

businesses and families in King's Cross [UK] as well as at our campsite in Wiltshire. We combine activities such as supporting bees, carpentry, urban food growing, cooking, and eating together with dialogue, story, creative writing, silence and stillness. These practices help us to create the conditions for people to come together in a fuller and more connected sense of who they are and what they are a part of and from that space, to support them to practically contribute to ecological and social change.

We have developed a methodology based around the three territories of 'I, We and the Planet' which is present in all the work that we do. This approach provides space for people to increase awareness of self, to connect to each other and to connect to the natural world. Whilst our activities are practical and hands on, bringing raw nature, elemental forces and a sense of adventure to the city, the work is grounded in values and widening of perspective to help establish a fertile foundation for growing a less consumerist and a more creative future.

Pop Culture Collaborative[58] [USA]

Established in 2016, the Pop Culture Collaborative is a philanthropic resource and funder learning community that uses grant making, convening, narrative strategy, and research to transform the narrative landscape around people of color, immigrants, refugees, Muslims, and Native people– especially those who are women, queer, transgender, and/or disabled. The Collaborative believes there is an opportunity– and that philanthropy has a responsibility– to build a field capable of shaping popular culture to reflect the complexity of the American people and make a just and pluralistic future feel real, desirable, and inevitable. Through partnerships between the social justice sector and the pop culture industries, the Collaborative believes activists, artists,

---

58 https://popcollab.org/about-us/

and philanthropists can encourage mass audiences to reckon with the past and rewrite the story of our nation's future.

Space2B[59] [Australia]

Space2b is an art & design social enterprise established to build a better future for newly arrived migrant & refugees: it offers an opportunity for newly arrived migrants to build on their traditional skills and knowledge, gain confidence and take their first steps on the path to financial independence. A safe space where the local community, local designers and artists and newly arrived migrant can come together to acquire business and creative skills, build relationships and make connections. A training centre to build creative, business and English-language skills. A platform for independent designers to develop their business, their product, and to showcase, promote and sell their work.

It is beyond the capacity of this book to insist that the Uniting Church become the prophetic voice that John might hope for. It is beyond its scope to offer a way forward for this to occur, except to say that it is needed. Without this prophetic calling, supporting and nurturing staff within the Uniting Agency, I suggest Uniting staff members' ability to practice negative capability, to sit comfortably in a liminal space and to learn to practise dadirri ...is limited. But I am hopeful that my account of John's experience in applying these practices in the workplace and in his personal life, and the concepts and the cycle of reflection I have offered here, may assist leaders and staff in Uniting and the wider church to begin the process of reflection, which may of itself lead some, perhaps to then call on the church to claim its place as a whole and holy people, faithful to their calling into the world for the sake of God's justice and righteousness.

---

59 https://space2b.com.au/

Reflections on the Material in this Chapter

This chapter summarises the iterative nature of the way John Bottomley created his reports, books and his views on our society and the place of the church in it. It notes the similarity of this deep listening with the Ignatian reflection cycle, the concept of negative capability (as coined by the poet John Keats) and the Aboriginal term dadirri. The Chapter offers a reflective cycle to help the reader to consider sitting quietly in times of work stress and allowing ideas to come from the liminal space beyond simplistic, binary notions.

- Is listening to the stories of clients always uppermost in your mind? What helps that to be so and what hinders it?
- What can you learn from your work with clients that gives you insight into the broader evils that exist in the world today?
- How important is religious faith in supporting decisions you take?
- What does having hope mean in your work, how it can be lived and how can it be given?
- Is there more that you can do? Or does the thought of 'doing more' simply make you feel exhausted? How can that be considered in a different way? Is there something you need to do less of?

CHAPTER 6

CONCLUDING THOUGHTS

I also will choose harsh treatment for them and will bring on them what they dread. For when I called, no one answered, when I spoke, no one listened. They did evil in my sight and chose what displeases me.
Isaiah 66:4

John Bottomley's work inside the Uniting Church and for the Creative Ministries Network came to an end in 2014 upon his retirement and the subsequent subsuming of the organisation into Uniting. But his work has not stopped there. In retirement, John tells me he has experienced a sense of freedom to write and speak on the issues of the church's abandonment of those suffering at the hands of the ideology (and idolatry) of hard work, both in Australia and in his missionary work in Sri Lanka.

He has found new colleagues through the Centre for Research in Religion and Social Policy (RASP) at the University of Divinity (formerly the Melbourne College of Divinity) which accredits all theological courses for most Christian denominations in Melbourne. Here he has found colleagues to work on new papers together, book chapters, speaking engagements, which take him to new places in getting his messages out. At RASP, John has contributed to the development of industry partnerships, published a paper drawing together principles for theological research from the lessons learned at CMN, is developing a research proposal to study the impact of the university work environment on University of Divinity academics, and made a submission for RASP offering a theological perspective on the interim report of the Royal Commission into banking.

John and his wife Margaret travel annually to Jaffna in Sri Lanka where they work with the Bishop of Jaffna and a local Christian school in Jaffna to bring much needed resources, ideas and action to an area still suffering the effects of twenty-five years of bloody civil war. They bring much needed policy development skills to the Diocese and the College, and John enjoys the opportunity to lead workshops with diocesan pastors on such topics as pastoral care, responding to trauma, and guiding the integration of their faith and daily work. John's research of Bishop Thiagrajah's life and ministry led to a co-authored book with the Bishop that was published in 2016 for the tenth anniversary of the Bishop's consecration.

John tells me it has taken him nearly four years to recover from the fact that the Creative Ministries Network and its programs are no longer integrated with the research, worship and theological enterprise of the former agency.

As the last Chairperson of CMN, I am also disappointed and I grieve that key elements of our legacy, including new ways of thinking, critiquing neoliberalism, linking worship and mission, new ways to work with those marginalised by workplace illness or injury and new forms of church seem (to me) to be ignored in the new structure. The focus on a mission to work – which was the focus of the work in CMN and its predecessor agencies, has not been taken up within Uniting. I also grieve for Uniting and the Synod, not only for what has been lost, but also for the possibilities for the church in Australia to bring these urgently needed perspectives to a nation that has turned its back on the root causes of so much pain and injustice in the world of work and economic life.

This book is not sufficient to capture the work of three decades. It is not enough to ensure the work goes on. It has taken me considerably longer than I anticipated to write this book, because I have struggled with the meaning and purpose of it. I have struggled to do justice to the themes in one slim volume all the while feeling the weight of the trauma of the loss of the agency, the loss of significant funds and the loss of focus on workplace research by the church.

I have moved back and forth over the two years it has taken to prepare this work between feeling despair and hopelessness about its purpose and audience, to rallying my energy to write more by either feeling anger at the loss of the focus of John's work in the Church, or by my loyalty to him to get the job done! I have thought of the loneliness of writing and the loneliness of working in a community service agency as having similar resonances. In the end I have been sustained by the hope that the struggle for justice has intrinsic worth, and the integrity of my struggle will be a strength to others.

We want things to be better than they are in the world. I have tried to offer ways of using John's words in practical daily contemplation rituals. But I wonder if it is enough. I worry that the quote above from Isaiah suggests that if we continue to turn away from each other and from caring for the earth that we will in fact bring on what we dread. I worry that in not speaking truth to power, that in accepting the inevitability of capitalism and the dominance of business language and thinking, that what we dread may already be upon us.

We survive each day and we do our best, but we don't believe anything can really change. We feel powerless to halt the decline into despair or to hedonism. We keep our fears locked up and private. We struggle to care for so many causes requiring our attention.

Recently, John said….

My reflection today is that my 'care' is more fruitful when I accept that I am powerless to 'fix' another person's suffering and enter into solidarity with them through deep listening to the pain in their story. The surprise for me has been to listen to the person recover their sense of agency and hope as their story is accepted and validated through my listening, and then critically, whether they wish to invite me to any further participation in their story. At that point, I believe we begin in a new relationship as peers, as equals in our common humanity.

As I finally finish writing the book, John reminded me of the parable of the scattered seeds from Matthew's gospel. I copy the story here. This is my hope in the writing of the book; that I can, in a small and heartfelt way, honour the work of my friend John Bottomley and show his significant body of work to a new audience. I am like the farmer scattering seeds in the fervent hope that some readers will gain a new perspective or reflect more deeply on their own work and direction in life. I want them to reflect down into their roots and perhaps take courage to go in a new direction that is truly what the world needs. I hope some readers can listen deeply without the lure of wealth or the worries of life crowding out the wellspring of dadirri and can draw on it for their own peace of mind and to act in the world. I want the seeds of the lessons described here to find good soil and grow.

Parable of the farmer scattering seed

"Listen! A farmer went out to plant some seeds. As he scattered them across his field, some seeds fell on a footpath, and the birds came and ate them. Other seeds fell on shallow soil with underlying rock. The seeds sprouted quickly because the soil was shallow. But the plants soon wilted under the hot sun, and since they didn't have deep roots, they died. Other seeds fell among thorns that grew up and choked out the tender plants. Still other seeds fell on fertile soil, and they produced a crop that was thirty, sixty, and even a hundred times as much as had been planted! Anyone with ears to hear should listen and understand."

Jesus' disciples came and asked him, "Why do you use parables when you talk to the people?" He replied, "You are permitted to understand the secrets of the Kingdom of Heaven, but others are not. To those who listen to my teaching, more understanding will be given, and they will have an abundance of knowledge. But for those who are not listening, even what little understanding they have will be taken away from them. That is why I use these parables,

For they look, but they don't really see.
They hear, but they don't really listen or understand.

This fulfils the prophecy of Isaiah that says,
'When you hear what I say,
you will not understand.
When you see what I do,
you will not comprehend.
For the hearts of these people are hardened,
and their ears cannot hear,
and they have closed their eyes—
so their eyes cannot see,
and their ears cannot hear,

and their hearts cannot understand,
and they cannot turn to me
and let me heal them.'

"But blessed are your eyes, because they see; and your ears, because they hear. I tell you the truth, many prophets and righteous people longed to see what you see, but they didn't see it. And they longed to hear what you hear, but they didn't hear it. Now listen to the explanation of the parable about the farmer planting seeds: The seed that fell on the footpath represents those who hear the message about the Kingdom and don't understand it. Then the evil one comes and snatches away the seed that was planted in their hearts. The seed on the rocky soil represents those who hear the message and immediately receive it with joy. But since they don't have deep roots, they don't last long. They fall away as soon as they have problems or are persecuted for believing God's word. The seed that fell among the thorns represents those who hear God's word, but all too quickly the message is crowded out by the worries of this life and the lure of wealth, so no fruit is produced. The seed that fell on good soil represents those who truly hear and understand God's word and produce a harvest of thirty, sixty, or even a hundred times as much as had been planted!"

Matthew 13:1-23

REFERENCES

Adorno T (1966) 'Education after Auschwitz' in *Critical Models. Interventions and Catchwords.* New York Columbia University Press 1998

Berman M (1982) *All that is Solid Melts into Air: The Experience of Modernity* Penguin New York

Bottomley JK &Tehan M (2002) *They don't know what to say or do: a research report on developing a best practice support model in the workplace for people with a life-threatening illness and employed carers* Palliative Care Victoria Melbourne Australia

Bottomley JK, Neith M & Dalziel E (2002) *Work Factors in Suicide: Evidence for a new commitment in occupational health and safety research, policy and practice* Urban Ministry Network Melbourne Australia

Bottomley JK (1997) *The Pressure is Enormous: the hidden costs of corporatisation* Union Research Centre on Organisation and Technology Melbourne, Australia

Bottomley JK (2015) *Hard Work Never Killed Anybody: how the idolisation of work sustains this deadly lie* Morning Star Publishing Northcote Australia

Bottomley JK & Wallace H (2007) *Risk Management in the New Heaven and the New Earth: Isaiah and UnitingCare Victoria and Tasmania's Corporate Governance Policy Melbourne College of Divinity [unpublished]*

Bottomley, JK in conversation with Deverell, G (2009) *Cannot be told before its time: a research project report into Aboriginal leadership in the Uniting Church, including a reflection on the need for repentance by research agencies captive to mainstream beliefs about science and truth* Creative Ministries Network Melbourne Australia

Bottomley JK & Neith M (2011) *Cutting Corners: Cleaners' Struggle For Justice With Victorian Shopping Centres' Contract Cleaning System* United Voice and Creative Ministries Network

Bridgman T, McLaughlin C & Cummings S (2018) 'Overcoming the Problem With Solving Business Problems: Using Theory Differently to Rejuvenate the Case Method for Turbulent Times' *Journal of Management Education* vol. 42(4) pp. 441-460

Bion WR (1961) *Experiences in Groups* London Tavistock.

Bion WR (1962) *Learning from Experience* London Heinemann

Bion, WR (1980) *Bion in New York and São Paulo* Perthshire Clunie Press

Brookes D (2008) *Restorative Justice and Work-related Death: a literature review* Melbourne Creative Ministries Network

Brookes D (2009)*Restorative Justice and Work-related Death: Consultation Report* Melbourne Creative Ministries Network

Brueggemann W (2015) (Hanson KC editor)*The God of All Flesh and Other Essays* Cascade Books Oregon

Burris V (1988) 'Reification: A Marxist Perspective' *California Sociologist* vol. 10(1) pp. 22-43

Chalcraft D (2001) 'Max Weber on the Watchtower: on the Prophetic Use of Shakespeare's Sonnet 102 in Politics as a Vocation' *Max Weber Studies* vol. 1(2) pp. 215-230

Crawley H & Skleparis D (2018) 'Refugees, migrants, neither, both: categorical fetishism and the politics of bounding in Europe's 'migration crisis' *Journal of Ethnic and Migration Studies* vol. 44(1) pp. 48-64

Cummins A (2002) 'The Road to Hell is Paved with Good Intentions: Quality Assurance as a Social Defence Against Anxiety.' *Organisation and Social Dynamics* vol. 2(1) pp. 99-119

Dempsey K & Bottomley JK (2011) 'Has God Stopped Calling or Has the Church Stopped Listening - Perspectives on the Decline and Regeneration of Ordained Ministry Candidates for the Uniting Church in Australia' *Socio-Analysis* No. 13 pp. 63-77

Du Gay P (2000) *In Praise of Bureaucracy*. Sage. London

Einstein A (1950) *Letter to Robert Marcus* In: A. Calaprice, (ed.) (2005) 'TheNew Quotable Einstein' NJ. Princeton University

Freud S (1930) *Civilization and its discontents* Oxford England Hogarth

Gabriel Y (1998) 'Psychoanalytic contributions to the study of the emotional life of organizations' *Administration & Society* Vol. 30(3) pp. 291-314

Gibbs G (1988) Learning by Doing: *A guide to teaching and learning methods* Further Education Unit Oxford Polytechnic Oxford

Glass D (2016) *Investigation into the management of complex workers compensation claims and WorkSafe oversight* Victorian Ombudsman Report Victorian Government Printer

Gooder H & Jacobs M (2000) 'On the border of the unsayable' *Interventions* 2 pp. 229–247

Goudzwaard R (1979) *Capitalism and Progress,* Trans. & edited by Josina Van Nuis Zylstra, English edition Wedge/ Eerdmans Michigan USA

Goudzwaard B (1984) *Idols of Our Time* Illinois Inter-varsity Press

Greenberg (2012) 'Kleinian Reparation: A Psychoanalytic
    Exploration of Residential School Apology in Canada'
    PhD [unpublished] University of Toronto Accessed 5th
    February 2019 at https://tspace.library.utoronto.ca/
    bitstream/1807/35082/3/Greenberg_Barbara_201211_
    Phd_thesis.pdf
Greenleaf R (1970) *The Servant as Leader*
    https://static1.squarespace.com/
    static/51473514e4b0090a1cad74f9/t/5194
    e399e4b0b0879dc2e8ef/1368712089353/
    Greenleaf+essay+part+one.pdf accessed 22.02.2019.
Harvey B (1999) *Another city: An ecclesiological primer for a post-
    Christian world* USA Trinity Press
House RJ & Aditya RN (1997) 'The Social Scientific Study of
    Leadership: Quo Vadis?'*Journal of Management* vol.
    23(3) pp. 409-473
Klein M (1935/1975) 'A Contribution to the Psychogenesis of
    Manic-Depressive States' Writings vol. 1 Free Press
    (Macmillan) NY Available at https://www.sas.upenn.
    edu/~cavitch/pdf-library/Klein_Contribution.pdf
Linossier P (1994) *A Common Sense of Purpose: The Rejoining of
    Word and Deed. Commission for Mission Uniting Church in
    Australia* [unpublished, provided by author]
Levine DP (2005) 'The fantasy of inevitability in organizations'
    Human Relations vol.51(10) pp. 1251-1265
Matthews LR, Quinlan M, Rawlings-Way O & Bohle P (2012) 'The
    Adequacy of Institutional Responses to Death at Work:
    Experiences of Surviving Families' International *Journal
    of Disability Management* vol.6 pp. 37–48
Mellor PA & Shilling C (1993) 'Modernity, Self-Identity and the
    Sequestration of Death' *Sociology* vol. 27(3) pp. 411-
    431

Middleton JR & Walsh BJ (1995) *Truth is stranger than it used to be: Biblical faith in a postmodern age* Intervarsity Press Illinois

Mishra P (2017) *Age of Anger* Penguin Random House UK

Naismith B (2017) *Death at Work* Available at www.ohsintros. com.au and accessed 20th March 2019

Neimeyer RA, Klass D & Dennis MR (2014) 'A social constructionist account of grief: loss and the narration of meaning' *Death Studies* vol. 38(6-10) pp. 485-498

Nouwen H (1979) *The Wounded Healer: Ministry in Contemporary Society* Doubleday NY

Parliamentary Joint Committee on Corporations and Financial Services (2019) *Fairness in Franchising* Commonwealth of Australia, Senate Printing Unit, Parliament House, Canberra.

Pollock S, Bottomley K & Taket A (ed. Nette A 2014) *Filling the Dark Spot, fifteen injured workers shine a light on the workers compensation system to improve it for others* Creative Ministries Network Melbourne Australia

Routley V & Ozanne-Smith J (2010) 'Work Related Suicide Stressors. Work Related Fatality project' *Department of Forensic Medicine Monash University*. Report No 1010-005-R4

Routley V Trytell G & Ozanne-Smith J (2011) 'Suicide and Work related stress in Victoria' *Department of Forensic Medicine Monash University Research Report* No 1111-005-R10

Sandel, M (2012) *What Money Can't Buy. The Moral Limits of Markets*. Penguin UK

Sennett R (1998) *The Corrosion of Character* Norton & Co. New York

Sennett R (2009) *The Craftsman* University Press Yale

Simpson P, French R and Harvey CE (2002) 'Leadership and negative capability' *Human Relations* vol. 55(10) pp.1209-1226

Smith KK (2003) 'A World Of Possibilities: Implications For Applied Behavioral Science' *Journal Of Applied Behavioral Science* vol. 39(4)

Stein HF & Allcorn S (2014) 'Good Enough Leadership: a Model of Leadership' *Organisational & Social Dynamics* vol.14 (2) pp. 342–366

Sutton S (2017) 'Who do we think we are? The myth of the individual mind' Presented at ACP Annual Conference 2017, London accessed 7th March 2019 at http://www. learning-studio.org/wp-content/uploads/Who-do-we-think-we-are-The-myth-of-the-individual-by-Dr-Sarah-Sutton.pdf

Ungunmerr-Baumann MR (2002) Dadirri: Inner Deep Listening and Quiet Still Awareness. Accessed 7th March 2019 at http://nextwave.org.au/wp-content/uploads/Dadirri-Inner-Deep-Listening-M-R-Ungunmerr-Bauman-Refl.pdf

Verhaeghe P (2012) 'Capitalism and psychology: identity and angst: on civilisation's new discontent' in Vermeersch (ed.), *The crisis comes in many guises* (pp. 55–63) Gerrit Kreveld Foundation and Samenlevingenpolitiek

Wallace H & Bottomley JK (2012) *Hope for Justice and Reconciliation* Morning Star Press, Northcote, Australia

Weber M (1905/1958) *The Protestant Work Ethic and the Spirit of Capitalism* Trans. Talcott Parsons as The Protestant Ethic and the Spirit of Capitalism New York Scribner's 1930 1958

Wetherell, JL (2012) 'Complicated grief therapy as a new treatment approach' *Dialogues in Clinical Neuroscience* 14(2) pp.159–16

Wilken, J (1992) 'A Theological Approach to Reconciliation,' in F. Brennan (ed.) *Reconciling our Differences: A Christian Approach to Recognising Aboriginal Land Rights,* Richmond, Victoria, Australia Aurora House 63-77

Wittkowski J, Doka KJ, Neimeyer RA & Vallerga M (2015) 'Publication Trends in Thanatology: An Analysis of Leading Journals' *Death Studies* vol.39 (8) 453-462

Wink W (1992) *Engaging the Powers: Discernment and Resistance in a World of Domination* Fortress Press Minneapolis MN

Wood E (1997) 'Modernity, Postmodernity or Capitalism?' *Review of International Political Economy* vol. 4 (3) pp. 539-556

JOHN BOTTOMLEY'S WORK HISTORY

1970-72 and 1982 –83 Part-time Research Worker, Centre for Urban Research and Action

1973	*Parish Worker, Uniting Church of Fitzroy*
1974-82	*Minister, Knox Methodist Circuit and Scoresby Uniting Church*
1984-85	*Research worker, Williamstown Naval Dockyard*
1985-1991	*Director, Urban Ministry Network*
1987	*Acting manager, Central Metropolitan Regional TAFE Board*
1991-2003	*Minister, East St Kilda Uniting Church Parish (part-time)*
1991-2004	*Director, Urban Ministry Network (part-time)*
2004-2013	*Director, Creative Ministries Network*
2013-2014	*Deputy Director, Creative Ministries Network*
2015	*Mission Co-worker, Jaffna Diocese, Church of South India (volunteer)*
2016	*Consultant, Transforming Work*

SELECTED HISTORY OF CREATIVE MINISTRY ACTIVITIES, PUBLICATIONS AND WORKSHOPS SPANNING THIRTY YEARS.

Publications

Arnold R, Bottomley JK, Harry, M & Page, C (2013) 'Trust at
 Work: how UnitingCare agency businesses serve
 God's mission: a research report on case studies at
 Connections, Prahran Mission, and Tasmania' Creative
 Ministries Network. Melbourne, Australia.

Bottomley JK (1988) 'We're all in the same boat: a literature
 review on the role of support groups for injured
 workers as a preventative measure in community
 mental health' Urban Ministry Network. Melbourne,
 Australia.

Bottomley JK & Sawtell J (1990) 'The Social Impact of Salinity on
 Farming Families in the Waranga and Deakin Shires'
 Goulburn Social Development Council. Australia.

Bottomley JK (1991) 'Footsteps Back to Living: creating
 your own rituals and ceremonies for death and
 bereavement' Urban Ministry Network. Melbourne,
 Australia.

Bottomley JK (1997) 'The Pressure is Enormous: the hidden
 costs of corporatisation' Union Research Centre on
 Organisation and Technology. Melbourne, Australia.

Bottomley JK (1998) 'Ministry in Working Life' Urban Ministry Network. Melbourne, Australia.

Bottomley JK (1998b) 'Widening Participation in ACE: Strategies for using the strength inherent in the cultural diversity of communities and individuals' Adult Community & Further Education Board. Melbourne, Australia.

Bottomley JK (2000) 'I think of him every day: transforming the grief of work-related death into renewed workplace safety' Urban Ministry Network. Melbourne, Australia.

Bottomley JK (2001) 'Bereavement Support Groups – issues in development, leadership, training' volume 1 Urban Ministry Network. Melbourne, Australia.

Bottomley JK (2001b) 'Developing Company Policy – practical advice for employers after a work-related death.' Volume 2 Urban Ministry Network. Melbourne, Australia.

Bottomley JK (2001c) 'Justice and Healing – spirituality and work-related death' Volume 3 Urban Ministry Network. Melbourne, Australia.

Bottomley JK &Neith M (2002) 'Literature review for Indigenous employment program' Urban Ministry Network. Melbourne, Australia.

Bottomley, JK &Neith, M (2011) 'Cutting Corners: Cleaners' Struggle For Justice With Victorian Shopping Centres' Contract Cleaning System'. United Voice and Creative Ministries Network.

Bottomley JK & Tehan M (2002) 'They don't know what to say or do: a research report on developing a best practice support model in the workplace for people with a life-threatening illness and employed carers.' Palliative Care Victoria. Melbourne, Australia.

Bottomley JK, Neith M & Dalziel E (2002) 'Work Factors in Suicide: Evidence for a new commitment in occupational health and safety research, policy and practice' Urban Ministry Network. Melbourne, Australia.

Box Hill Institute of TAFE. (2003) 'It's Your Life: Renewing workplace safety for young Australians' (DVD) Urban Ministry Network. Melbourne, Australia.

Bottomley JK (2004) 'Treated Like a Leper, a survey of companies prosecuted after a work-related death' Creative Ministries Network. Melbourne, Australia.

Bottomley JK (2007) 'Towards a Charter: developing a partnership between Uniting Church Schools and other parts of the Uniting Church in the Synod of Victoria and Tasmania' Commission for Mission, Synod of Victoria and Tasmania. Melbourne, Australia.

Bottomley JK (2007) 'Towards a renewed vision for Uniting Church prison ministry: a report based on prison chaplains work integrating social analysis and theological reflection' [unpublished] Creative Ministries Network. Melbourne, Australia.

Bottomley JK (2007b) Briefing paper to the Executive Director of the Synod Property Trust on the impact of a regulation to authorise Presbyteries to declare congregational property 'available for alternative missional use.' Creative Ministries Network. Melbourne, Australia.

Bottomley JK (ed.) (2007c) 'Simple and Quiet Sisters: peace and love require no arms: multi-faith perspectives on peace' Creative Ministries Network. Melbourne, Australia.

Bottomley JK (2008) 'In, but not of the world: a report on issues to strengthen the faith and vocation of UnitingCare

CEOs, officers, Boards and agencies' Creative Ministries Network. Melbourne, Australia.

Bottomley JK (2008b) 'Project Report: Towards meeting the spiritual needs of people with disabilities resident in Wesley Disability Support Eastern' Creative Ministries Network. Melbourne, Australia.

Bottomley JK (2009) 'Death, illness and grief: foundational mysteries for transforming and humanizing work', a chapter in *Promoting Workplace Wellbeing* (2009) Thompson, N, Bates,es, J (eds) Palgrave Macmillan UK.

Bottomley JK (2009) Working on the church's margins '"What's love got to do with it?" Grief in Australian Workplaces' *Grief Matters* Summer, Vol. 12, No. 3. Australian Centre for Grief and Bereavement. Melbourne, Australia.

Bottomley, JK in conversation with Deverell, G. (2009) 'Cannot be told before its time: a research project report into Aboriginal leadership in the Uniting Church, including a reflection on the need for repentance by research agencies captive to mainstream beliefs about science and truth' Creative Ministries Network. Melbourne, Australia.

Bottomley, JK & Neith M (eds) (2009) 'Like Streams in a Dry Place: reflections on the Network's 25 years' Creative Ministries Network' Creative Ministries Network Melbourne, Australia.

Bottomley, JK & Neith M. (2010) 'Work and Suicide: the need for improved data collection on work factors in suicide as a contribution to suicide prevention' Creative Ministries Network. Melbourne, Australia.

Bottomley JK (2011) 'Discussion Paper: Mission and Ministry at work' Creative Ministries Network. Melbourne, Australia.

Bottomley JK (2011b) 'Spirit of Yearning, spirit of service: encouraging spiritual discernment and spiritual formation in mental health ministry' for Yarra Yarra Presbytery. Creative Ministries Network. Melbourne, Australia.

Bottomley JK (2015) 'Hard Work Never Killed Anybody: how the idolisation of work sustains this deadly lie'. Morning Star Publishing. Northcote, Australia

Bottomley JK (2015b) 'Our system isn't geared for death: theological and sociological reflections on the narratives of ten women widowed by their husband's work-related death and their experience on workers' compensation.' Creative Ministries Network. Melbourne, Australia.

Brookes D (2008) 'Restorative Justice and Work-related Death: a literature review' Creative Ministries Network. Melbourne, Australia.

Brookes D (2009) 'Restorative Justice and Work-related Death: Consultation Report' Creative Ministries Network. Melbourne, Australia.

Brookes D (2011) 'Restorative Justice after a traumatic death: Quality Assurance Framework for a Pilot Restorative Justice Service' Creative Ministries Network. Melbourne, Australia

Dempsey, K & Bottomley JK (2011) 'Has God Stopped Calling or Has the Church Stopped Listening - Perspectives on the Decline and Regeneration of Ordained Ministry Candidates for the Uniting Church in Australia' *Socio-Analysis* No. 13 pp. 63-77

Dempsey, K & McMillan L (2015) It's Never Ending, It's Ceaseless ...A Business Series Report. Reventure Ltd. Queensland, Australia

Jennings A (2006) 'Time Lost: getting through grief.' Creative Ministries Network. Melbourne, Australia.

Koller V (2000) 'Sick-leave survey for Waterfront Workers' Urban Ministry Network. Melbourne, Australia.

Mobayad E (1998) 'Til Death us do Part: industrial death narratives' Urban Ministry Network. Melbourne, Australia.

New Areas Ministry Team (2012) 'Christ's Call to New Areas of Ministry: a report from the New Areas Ministry Team.' Creative Ministries Network. Melbourne, Australia.

Pearce B & Pearce S, (2007) 'Geelong to Nui Dat and Back.' Creative Ministries Network. Melbourne, Australia.

Pollock, S, Bottomley, J &Taket A, (ed. Nette A) (2014) 'Filling the Dark Spot, fifteen injured workers shine a light on the workers compensation system to improve it for others. Creative Ministries Network. Melbourne, Australia

Wallace, H & Bottomley JK (2008) 'Risk management in God's new heaven and new earth: Isaiah's vision of judgment for UnitingCare Victoria and Tasmania's corporate governance policy' *Uniting Church Studies* United Theological College. Sydney Australia

Wallace, H & Bottomley JK (2011) 'Hope for Justice and Reconciliation: Isaiah's voice in an Australian context' Uniting Academic Press Northcote, Australia

Winja Art Program participants 'Winja Stories' (revised edition) (2003) Stories, songs and artwork from the Urban Dreaming Project participants Centre for Creative Ministries. Melbourne. Australia.

Liturgical Services, Exhibitions and Workshops

- Suicide Prevention Forum: can we do more to save lives 2016
- Established the Victorian Truck Drivers Memorial Service in cooperation with the Alexandra Truck, Ute and Rod Show. The remembrance service honours the men and women who have died while doing their work. 2013
- Conducted a self-care workshop for paramedics 2013
- Developed three pilot projects on mission and ministry at work. The Synod project was a roundtable conversation integrating faith and work; the congregation project was a collegiate group for three congregational ministers supporting their ministry with work issues. The agency project comprised three case studies with UnitingCare agencies on doing God's business. 2012
- Rev Jackson Day, a US Vietnam Veteran and member of the US-based International Conference of War Veteran Ministers, was brought to Melbourne by CMN. Rev Jackson was guest speaker at the first CMN Remembrance Eve dinner, preached at Wesley UC and St Paul's Cathedral for Remembrance Sunday, led a one-day workshop on 'Spiritual wounds and mental health' at the CTM, met with two Indigenous people to inform his United Methodist conversations with native Americans, shared in a hospitality dinner with Sri Lankan Bishop Daniel Thiagarajah, and attended Contemplative Worship at Geelong followed by a Vietnam Veterans Geelong branch barbeque. 2012

- Workshops on grief support for volunteer staff at a UnitingCare agency and teachers at UC schools. 2012
- Director interviewed on work factors in suicide for ABC TVs '7.30', and for ABC Radio National 'Encounter'. 2012
- Workshop for the Bereavement Support Groups Network on 'staff wellbeing'. 2012
- Timber Workers Memorial Service was conducted with support from a funeral company. 2012
- Six people completed a five-day training program in restorative justice in 2010
- A theology student completed placement in 2010
- Co-sponsored a visit from Bishop Daniel Thiagarajah of Jaffna Diocese. He led a Bible study for veterans on forgiveness for those hurt by war, trauma and violence. 2009
- An exhibition of Lorraine Austin's art work formed by meetings with veterans was held at the CTM 2009
- Exhibition of Winja Ulupna women's art at the Australian Catholic University Gallery, and then at Ivanhoe Uniting Church from Easter to Pentecost 2009
- A seminar on 'Grief @ work' for the Australian Centre for Grief and Bereavement 2009
- A workshop with the Board and CEO of Kilmany UnitingCare to assist their work on 'governance and faith' 2009
- Bi-monthly professional development workshops facilitated for UC prison chaplains in 2008
- A program of workshop sessions for ministers in UC community service agencies with the Centre for Theology and Ministry

- Koori Artist-in-residence in our Aboriginal Access Art Studio 2007
- Lecturing in OHS at Holmesglen TAFE 2007
- Veterans' song writing project. Contemplative Worship for veterans once per month at All Saints Anglican Church in Newtown 2007
- Five choirs, a kyoto player and an origami workshop leader contributed to the peace concert 'Sing War No More' to mark the 60th anniversary of the atomic bomb dropped on Hiroshima. A donation was forwarded to the Japanese National Council of Churches for its ministry with children affected by radiation poisoning. 2006
- Contemplative Worship for Vietnam Veterans commenced in Geelong in 2006
- Offered field education supervision for a theological student 2005
- Commenced telephone support for the social justice work of Gippsland Asbestos Related Diseases Support (GARDS). This monthly support continued until 2014
- Preach at Ivanhoe UC during the five Sundays of Lent on 'God's work, our work' 2005
- 'They don't know what to say or do' workshop for VECCI on responding to the needs of staff and workers with a life-threatening illness. 2005
- Commenced Contemplative Worship two Sunday evenings per month 2005
- Grief support to four companies: one where a worker was killed, one where the MD died from a heart attack, the third where a worker committed suicide in the factory, and the fourth where the owner's son died in a car accident. 2004

- 'Nurturing nurses 'being' art therapy workshop series for nurses at Epworth Hospital. 2004
- 'Leadership as calling and task' workshop for management training at the Alfred Hospital. 2004
- 'Chaplaincy as calling and gift' workshop for UCA chaplains in hospitals, schools, prisons. 2004
- 'Recovery from a work-related death' workshop with AI Group and VECCI for their industry members. 2004
- CCM completed the Urban Dreaming Project, comprising a music program with Aboriginal men and women resident in alcohol and drug recovery houses, an art program and a successful tour of six Aboriginal drug and alcohol recovery centres in rural and regional Victoria. 2003
- Sponsored a final year social work student placement at the MUA 1999
- Two programs for men in management at a university on "Men's health and well-being" in response to the suicide of a manager. 1999
- Speaker at The ACTU's National Occupational Health and Safety Conference on "Changing Stress at Work".
- Conference speaker for Managers and CEOs of host companies in Group Training Australia (Vic.).
- Volunteers Grief Support Training Program for eleven volunteers
- CCM curated the exhibition Faith Works! at the National Gallery of Victoria 1998
- Provision of support for Women of the Waterfront Network through a series of small group and planning meetings during the Patrick dispute with the MUA. 1998

- Piloted a Professional and Faith Development Round Table for CEOs in church community service agencies with Lonergan Enterprises. 1998
- Arts & Christianity Conference 1993
- Workers' Memorial Service at Melbourne's Wesley Uniting Church. 1990
- Churches and Unions Working for Social Justice seminar 1988
- Auspice, Commissioned Work and Publishing Activities
- Professional photographer Shelley Morris was supported to mount an exhibition of photographs of victims of the civil war in Sri Lanka, with funds donated to JDCSI. 2013
- 'Healing the wounds of war' DVD for the 2012 Memorial Service to commemorate the 70th anniversary of the Kokoda campaign.
- Recognised the service of Barry Pearce with 'The Barry Pearce Peace Memorial Lecture to be held at the annual Remembrance Eve dinner for veterans and their families'. A Trust to organise and fund the lecture was appointed and the Board donated $5000 to establish the Trust Fund. 2013
- Commencement of the Veterans Chaplaincy Service (Rev. John Phillips) 2012
- Supported a volunteer to initiate the first Suicide Prevention Awareness Network walk in Bendigo
- Prophet and Loss, the DVD, was launched at ACMI. Rev. Peter Burnham developed an education package to support use of the DVD with congregations. 2011

- Contributed $125 to the prize for a nurse's essay on 'Encounter with Spirit' for an International Nurses Day service at St George's 2010
- Profit and Loss employed a talented cast and enjoyed a successful season over a two-week period with the final three sessions sold out. The final session opened the Centre for Theology and Ministry (CTM) Wisdom's Feast conference 2009
- Two WGS clients worked with Energy Safe Victoria to develop a DVD to educate farmers and others on safety with overhead power-lines 2009
- Published Rev. Peter Sanders' book of poetry *I brought my lunch*. 2009
- Palawa woman, Lorraine Austin, was appointed as Indigenous artist in residence for a visual art project with Vietnam Veterans in 2008
- *The Shark in the Fishbowl*. Script development and play-reading on workplace bullying 2008
- *Geelong to Nui Dat and Back* was written by Barry and Sandra Pearce and published as a creative writing project 2007
- Composer Sean Nihill completed the second movement of 'Kingsbury VC', a composition for Brass Band commissioned to support the annual St George's Uniting Church Memorial Service 2007
- Published Nick Randall's original compositions in *Contemplative Music volume 1: Beneath the Noise* as a valuable resource for participatory meditative worship.
- Creative writer mentored a client in a project that led to the publication of her story, *Just Work: an autobiographical account of workplace bullying.*

- Published Revd Paul Mayfield's poetry, Soul cry, Call Song at Ivanhoe UC. 2005
- Dedication of a Memorial Quilt for work-related deaths.
- Songwriter and composer Jennie Swain wrote 'Tell me' as a commissioned song for the Partnerships in Grieving Program (PIGP). 2003
- Published Jenni Mitchell's book, *Karen Kathleen: a healing narrative.* 1999

www.ingramcontent.com/pod-product-compliance
Lightning Source LLC
Chambersburg PA
CBHW060034030426
42334CB00019B/2322